SO-BBE-887

Lorenzo de Zavala

Manuel Lorenzo Justiniano de Zavala y Sáenz,
1788-1836 (courtesy Archives Division, Texas
State Library, Austin).

Lorenzo de Zavala

The Pragmatic Idealist

MARGARET SWETT HENSON

Texas Christian University Press
Fort Worth

Lorenzo de Zavala is Number One in the
"Significant Texans: Informal Biographies" Series

Copyright © 1996, Margaret Swett Henson

Library of Congress Cataloging-in-Publication Data

Henson, Margaret Swett, 1924-
    Lorenzo de Zavala : the pragmatic idealist / Margaret Swett
Henson.
        p. cm. — (Significant Texans ; no. 1)
    Includes bibliographical references and index.
    ISBN 0-87565-150-X (cloth). — ISBN 0-87565-151-8 (pbk.)
    1. Zavala, Lorenzo de, 1788-1836. 2. Vice-
Presidents—Texas—Biography. 3. Texas—History—Republic, 1836-
1846. 4. Statesmen—Texas—Biography. I. Title. II. Series.
F390.z4h46 1996
976.4'03'092—dc20
[B]
                                                    95-32720
                                                    CIP

Design by Barbara Whitehead

Contents

For Rolando Romo and
members of the Lorenzo de Zavala Chapter,
Tejano Association for Historic Preservation
Houston, Texas

Preface

THIS STUDY of Lorenzo de Zavala, the Yucatán-born signer of the Texas Declaration of Independence and the first vice president of the Republic of Texas, is written primarily for readers in Texas. Nevertheless, four of the seven chapters focus on Zavala's experiences in Mexico, a focus necessary to explain the forces that shaped this complicated man.

With this in mind, Mexican events that affected Texas and Zavala's political development are discussed as succinctly as possible. Thus the narrative is not an in-depth analysis of Spanish and Mexican politics between 1810 and 1836.

I acknowledge a great debt to the pioneer biographer of Zavala, Dr. Raymond Estep, whose 1942 doctoral dissertation at the University of Texas provides the details of Zavala's career in Mexico. Estep's study was published in Spanish in Mexico City in 1952, but Texans have been without a convenient full-length biography of Zavala. Books and articles published since Estep's seminal work and collections of primary material then unavailable have provided more details for the present study.

My interest in Zavala began in 1989 when Rolando Romo, the first president of Houston's Tejano Association for Historic Preservation, asked me to speak about the Yucatecan. The Houston group had chosen to name their chapter after Zavala, Harris County's first and most prominent Hispanic resident. Beyond that group, Zavala is modestly remembered locally by two schools, a road, and historic markers at his homesite on Buffalo Bayou and across the waterway at the San Jacinto Battleground.

Technological progress since 1913 has seriously damaged

the former Zavala property; dredging the bayou for the Houston Ship Channel and extracting subsurface water for industries resulted in bank erosion and six to nine feet of land settling. The site remained private property until 1939 when the United States acquired it for an arsenal; in 1964 it was sold for industrial purposes. The endangered headstones in the Zavala cemetery were moved to the battleground in 1968 by the Texas Parks and Wildlife Department, with the consent of descendants.

Perhaps this book will help revive wider interest in Zavala.

Margaret Swett Henson

Introduction

LORENZO DE ZAVALA was an intellectual, non-conformist, iconoclast willing to take risks to achieve his republican goals. Elected a delegate to the convention at Washington-on-the-Brazos by his Harrisburg neighbors, he signed the Texas Declaration of Independence on March 2, 1836, along with fifty-eight others including two Tejanos from San Antonio. He was the only delegate present who had previous experience writing a constitution for a republic and who had held office at both the national and state levels. He had also represented his neighborhood earlier at the November 1835 Consultation. Fellow delegates at Washington-on-the-Brazos unanimously named him vice president of the new Republic of Texas, expecting to attract Tejano support.

Born in Yucatán the same year that the new United States adopted its constitution, Zavala admired the government created by the men in Philadelphia. Between 1822 and 1824, he helped create a similar republic for Mexico and served in its first Congress. Later, as governor of the State of Mexico, he instituted reforms in education and land redistribution to improve the conditions of the Indians. In doing so, he antagonized the wealthy landowners, including the Roman Catholic Church. When he served as secretary of the treasury in 1829, he applied stringent financial measures to rescue the Mexican economy, a step that also angered the elite. A coup d'etat by reactionary centralists forced Zavala and fellow liberal federalists to seek sanctuary in the United States in 1830; there he observed Jacksonian democracy and entrepreneurial capitalism firsthand.

After two years in exile, Zavala resumed his governorship in Mexico when a second coup restored the federalists to power. As a reward for his service, he was named Mexico's first minister to the French court in 1833. But when President Santa Anna began dismantling the 1824 constitution, Zavala resigned in protest. Fearful for his life, he moved his family to Mexico's frontier state of Texas where he owned land. The Yucatecan also hoped to unite Anglo Texans with federalist rebels to remove Santa Anna from office. Anglo Texans, however, had their own agenda and the federalist scheme ultimately failed.

Zavala's brief sixteen months in Texas, during a time of great confusion, were a frustrating challenge for a seasoned politician. The universal acceptance he had encountered in the more cosmopolitan cities of Europe and the United States had not prepared Zavala for the xenophobic prejudice prevalent among many Anglo Texans. Moreover, as vice president he believed his talents were not utilized and his advice unheeded. Suffering recurring bouts with fever after reaching Texas, he died at his home opposite the San Jacinto Battleground on November 15, 1836. He was only forty-eight years old.

Mexican historians view Zavala with mixed emotions. Some praise his efforts to create a republic in Mexico and to improve the conditions of the lower classes. However, most see him as a traitor because he signed the Texas Declaration of Independence. In their eyes, his act led to the dismembering of the nation—the loss of California, Nevada, Utah, Arizona, New Mexico and a portion of Colorado—by the 1848 Treaty of Guadalupe Hidalgo that ended the war between Mexico and the United States. Only in his native Yucatán, known for its independent course in relation to the other Mexican states, is he considered a hero.

Texans, then and now, have made little effort to understand Zavala. A few cosmopolitan contemporaries admired his mind and political talents, but most suspected his motives.

Was he in Texas to further his land speculations? Was he cynically using Texans to further his presidential aspirations in Mexico? Anglo historians have generally ignored Zavala except for brief references to his vice presidency and footnotes in standard histories.

Evaluating Zavala's character and personality is difficult. The few surviving primary documents are colored by politics or self-serving rhetoric. Instead, the man must be judged by his acts. An idealistic republican, Zavala helped create two republics within a dozen years. In Mexico he was a republican reformer striving to end traditional privileges of the elite and empower the criollo middle class; in Texas, he sought economic stability for his family and hoped to restore his political career. His early death defeated both plans. Although the men at Washington-on-the-Brazos would have achieved their goal without him, his wise counsel in drafting a national constitution was an important contribution to Texas, as was his ability as a conciliator.

CHAPTER *1*

A Mission
to Texas in 1835

A GRACEFUL, WELL-DRESSED MAN in his mid-forties stood at the rail of the schooner *San Felipe* on July 7, 1835, while the steamboat nudged it away from the crowded wharf in New Orleans. The steamboat crew tied the *San Felipe* alongside other out-bound vessels and the flotilla started downstream to the Gulf of Mexico. The schooner, owned by New Orleans merchants engaged in the Texas cotton trade, was registered in Mexico and commanded by Captain William A. Hurd. With its large central cabin for dining and lounging plus a few small first-class staterooms, the *San Felipe* could carry sixty passengers while its hold would accommodate over two hundred compressed bales of cotton or an equal amount of freight.

Señor Lorenzo de Zavala, lately Mexican minister to the French court, was bound for Texas for the first time and looked forward to reaching the cool breezes of the Gulf. He had spent only a few days in steamy New Orleans meeting with other Mexican federalists, all political refugees, to discuss plans to force Mexican President Antonio Lopez de Santa Anna from office.

Zavala had recently resigned his diplomatic post in Paris after writing a violent attack against Santa Anna's increasingly dictatorial course that was changing the Mexican Republic into a centralized authoritarian nation. This denunciation made him a target for reprisal from his onetime friend. In fact, the president had ordered Zavala to report to Mexico City; instead he was sailing to Texas.

The Yucatán native had left Le Havre in April to join his wife and children who had preceded him to New York. After the birth of his third son in May, Zavala left his family to go to the Mexican frontier state of Texas. Although he had never been to Texas, he owned large tracts of undeveloped land acquired through profitable speculation. Thus his journey was for both economic and political reasons.

Fellow passengers on board the *San Felipe* found Zavala a congenial, cosmopolitan gentleman who spoke good English. During the four- to five-day voyage from Louisiana to the mouth of the Brazos River, they probably discovered that he was an articulate intellectual and an idealistic republican. The manners of the times, however, would have prevented Zavala from detailing the many political offices he had held in Mexico.

Sailing across the Gulf of Mexico toward Texas allowed Zavala time to contemplate his immediate mission. His federalist friends in New Orleans recognized his ability to mingle with Anglo American residents in Texas and they hoped that he would find support for a plan to destroy Santa Anna's regime. Elected president in 1833, the once-popular general at first posed as a federalist reformer to defeat the authoritarian centralist administration imposed by a coup d'etat in 1829. By 1834, however, President Santa Anna abandoned the federalists who had brought him to office and instead embraced the powerful and wealthy centralist faction. He recently had dismantled republican reforms aimed at the clergy and the military and had begun demolishing federalist-minded state governments.

Zavala was confident that his powers of persuasion would secure federalist support in Texas. He already knew that New Orleans merchants and their counterparts in Texas were angry because of the recent resumption of tariff collection in Texas ports. The colonization laws passed by the Mexican Congress in 1823 had provided a six-year exemption from import duties to Anglo Texans to encourage immigration. When the privilege expired, the Anglo Texans objected violently and won an extension. Santa Anna, however, needed revenue for his military campaigns and sent collectors and troops to assist them to Texas ports in January 1835.

Friends had assured Zavala that Anglo Texans would welcome the federalist plan to overthrow Santa Anna. Two months earlier, a Mexican armed vessel patrolling between Galveston Bay and the Brazos River had seized two Texas-owned schooners that were without Mexican customs clearance papers. This had caused a great deal of unrest in Texas.

Unknown to Zavala and his fellow conspirators at the time of his departure, an armed attack against the Mexican garrison at Anahuac on upper Galveston Bay had already occurred. William Barret Travis had led a few volunteers to Anahuac and captured the forty-member garrison on June 30. The purpose of the attack was twofold: to vent anger over the recent seizure of the vessels and the arrest of a local merchant and, more importantly, to seize the garrison before it could be reinforced. The Anglos had just captured a military courier bound for Anahuac with a dispatch indicating that additional troops were being sent to all Texas military posts. The presence of a standing army aroused Anglo Texans whose fathers and grandfathers had opposed the presence of British troops in the seaboard colonies.

Many conservative Texans, however, disapproved of Travis' precipitous action and feared that it might delay the release of

Stephen F. Austin, who was still a political prisoner in Mexico City. Austin had taken petitions for political and judicial reforms desired by the Texans to the capital in 1833. After many delays he penned an injudicious letter to San Antonio officials that caused his arrest and incarceration. Travis, aware that his campaign was not universally popular, sailed with his captives to Harrisburg en route to San Felipe, the seat of the District of the Brazos, where officials would decide what to do with the officers and men. Travis and the troops marched to San Felipe about the same time Zavala landed at the mouth of the Brazos.

Stephen F. Austin was one of the two Texans Zavala knew before this voyage. Zavala had met Austin in Mexico City in 1823 and again ten years later. The other was David G. Burnet, who lived on upper Galveston Bay. In 1830, Burnet and Zavala had both been in New York City where they sold their respective Mexican empresario grants to investors known as the Galveston Bay and Texas Land Company. Zavala still held company scrip for land located east of the Trinity River.

As he sailed toward Texas, Zavala also carried introductory letters from his federalist friends to merchant Thomas F. McKinney and other prominent Texans. A longtime trader with towns south of the Rio Grande, McKinney owned a commission house at the mouth of the Brazos River and an interest in the *San Felipe*. Word in New Orleans was that McKinney would be especially sympathetic to federalist goals since it was his schooner *Columbia* that had been seized and confiscated in May.

As the *San Felipe* neared the low, flat Texas coast, Zavala was surprised by the lack of vegetation on the barrier islands and peninsulas. Not even palm trees grew here as along the Mexican coast; Galveston Island had only three clumps of trees to serve as a landmark for passing mariners. Moreover, the government policy prohibiting foreign-born persons from occupying coastal lands except between the Brazos and

Colorado rivers in Austin's colony made the Texas coast appear deserted.

The *San Felipe* finally approached the mouth of the Brazos River where a dangerous shifting sandbar threatened vessels drawing more than five feet of water. Portions of four wrecked vessels lay along the long, wide sandbar—a disturbing sight for passengers. A pilothouse on the eastern bank flew signals telling vessels whether to await the arrival of a pilot. Ships often had to anchor offshore several days to wait for favorable wind and tides rather than risk taking passengers through the surf in lighters. Besides the pilothouse, there were a few scattered shacks, a ramshackle hotel, a saltworks, and the remains of a small fortification built in 1831 on the eastern shore.

The *San Felipe* eased over the bar safely and anchored slightly upriver at the McKinney and Williams warehouse located on a protective bend along the west bank. The partners had begun the town of Quintana in 1834, and when Zavala arrived, there were several small dwellings. McKinney and his wife occupied a large house elevated on piers because of high tides. This home also served as a guest house for travelers. Besides the commodious warehouse, there was a cotton gin and compress and a boatyard with a small schooner in progress.

A distant slave barracoon disturbed Zavala. He later learned that in May it had been full of newly arrived Africans who had been brought from Cuba in violation of Mexican law. Nevertheless, McKinney had allowed the smuggler to build the camp near the beach. Mexican idealists like Zavala disapproved of the African trade and American-style slavery in principle, but they pragmatically allowed Anglo Texans to bring their own domestic slaves in order to encourage the development of the cotton culture.

McKinney and his wife welcomed Zavala to their home, and the two men spoke at length about recent events. The news of Zavala's arrival quickly spread up the river to San Felipe. Captain Antonio Tenorio, formerly in command at

Anahuac, had just arrived there with Travis. On July 15, the captain wrote to Colonel Domingo de Ugartechea, his superior in San Antonio de Bexar, that the fugitive Zavala was at the mouth of the Brazos. Four days later, Ugartechea sent an order to the captain to arrest Zavala and bring him to Bexar. When Ugartechea's letter reached San Felipe on July 25, Zavala's new friends offered him protection. Tenorio told his commander that arresting Zavala was impossible without a stronger force. Thus began a long and unsuccessful effort to send Zavala to Mexico City.

What sort of man was this Yucatán native? How had he risen in politics to inspire such a manhunt? What drove Zavala to Texas when he could have remained in the United States? The answers to these questions lie in Zavala's heritage, education, idealism, and ambition.

CHAPTER 2

An Insurgent
During the
Viceroyalty
of New Spain

MANUEL Lorenzo Justiniano de Zavala y Sáenz, the fifth of nine children and the second son, was born on October 3, 1788, in Tecoh, a small village near Mérida, Yucatán. His parents, Anastasio de Zavala y Velásquez and María Bárbara Sáenz y Castro, took their newborn to Mérida one month later to be baptized in the massive old cathedral. Located on the east side of the principal plaza, the main portion of Nuestra Señora de la Encarnación had been finished in 1598; however, work on the impressive building continued almost to the time of little Lorenzo's baptism.

Mérida, Yucatán's capital, was established in 1542 on the site of an ancient Mayan town. Conquistador Francisco de Montejo y León destroyed the old pyramids and buildings and used the rubble for new construction. The city with its orderly grid of streets and plazas and its beautiful buildings was an inspirational environment for young Zavala. At an early age he became interested in the Mayan ruins at nearby

Uxmal (A.D. 600-900) and in the 1830s often spoke and wrote about the site.

Young Zavala's parents were criollos, Spaniards of Basque descent born in the colonies. (In Basque, Zavala means "wide.") Lorenzo's grandfather, Simón Felipe Antonio de Zavala y Marín, was born in Yucatán in 1725 soon after his father, José, had moved to the peninsula from Peru. Simón became a notary, not a mere witness of documents but a legal representative in Spanish-speaking countries. Thus, Lorenzo was a third-generation Yucatecan.

Lorenzo could have traced his ancestry back seven generations if he could have located baptismal and marriage records. Grandfather Simón's father, José Casimiro de Zavala y Ramírez, born in Peru, was a lawyer connected with the royal council in Yucatán. José's father was an immigrant to the New World: Don Antonio de Zavala y Leicaola, a captain of cavalry and a Caballero de la Orden de Santiago, married Isabel Ramírez in Peru in 1676. He had come from the village of Mendaro in the Spanish province of Guipúzcoa on the Bay of Biscay where his father and grandfather were born and died. Guipúzcoa is Basque country at the foot of the Pyrenees that separate France from Spain.

Echoing the sentiments of their forebears in Europe, both the Yucatecan Basques and the Spaniards were noted for their independent spirit and isolationism. (Modern-day Basques, in fact, remain aloof from Spain and continue to speak their own language.) The geography of the Basque country in Spain discouraged outsiders, and pilgrims making their way from Europe to the tomb of St. James (Santiago) at Campostela in extreme northwestern Spain made an arc around the area. The same can be said of the Yucatán. Isolated geographically, residents of the peninsula depended on water transportation to connect with the rest of Mexico, and were governed by a captain-general who exerted almost autonomous control independent of the viceroy. In the nineteenth century, Yucatán twice declared itself independent from Mexico.

Lorenzo de Zavala clearly was a product of this independent mind-set. Nothing is known about the home in which he grew up or even whether the family lived in Mérida, on a country estate, or both. The education he received, however, is better documented; it laid the foundation for his anticlericalism and his admiration for republican government.

An unusually bright youth, Zavala learned to read and write at an early age and in his teens became a boarding student in the Seminario Conciliar de San Ildefonso in Mérida. Also known as the Franciscan Tridentine seminary, it was the only school of higher learning in Yucatán and had been in existence since 1751. In this setting, Zavala excelled in most subjects and mastered Latin. One of his classmates was Andrés Quintana Roo; one year older than Zavala and the son of a wealthy Mérida family, he became a noted jurist and poet in Mexico City after Mexico declared its independence from Spain. In 1802 the pair studied philosophy with Don Pablo Moreno, an iconoclast for his times, who urged students to question traditional doctrines until proven. Zavala had met his mentor.

A story, perhaps apocryphal, is told about one occasion when fifteen-year-old Zavala publicly debated a tradition-bound teacher at the seminary who cited Thomas Aquinas as his authority:

"Do you deny the authority of the Divine Thomas?" challenged the priest.

"And why not?" replied the audacious youth. "Saint Thomas was human just as you and I, and could as easily have erred."

Zavala applied Moreno's principles to physical science and eventually to politics. His parents wanted him to study for the priesthood and he dutifully listened to lectures on moral and scholastic theology and read Latin discourses. One day he discovered a cache of nontraditional books in the seminary library, perhaps confiscated by officers of the Inquisition. (The Spanish Inquisition was a quasi-ecclesiastical tribunal established in 1478 by King Ferdinand and Queen Isabella to examine the sincerity of Jews and Muslims who had converted to Catholicism. The harsh punishment for polygamy, usury, and other crimes lessened by the seventeenth century, but the monarch found the institution useful in the eighteenth century to stamp out the threatening ideas of the Enlightenment.)

Some of the books Zavala found were in French, and he immediately set to work learning that language. While he had heard of Galileo, Newton, Locke, Montesquieu, Rousseau, and other philosophers of the age, he had been unable to read any of their works because they were banned by the Spanish authorities. Later he wrote about his seminary training: "No useful truth, no principle, no axiom capable of inspiring noble or generous sentiments was heard...."

In 1807, at the age of nineteen, his formal education ended because his family lacked money to send him to the university in Mexico City where Quintana Roo would study. One year later, Lorenzo married Teresa Josefa Correa y Correa. She was the thirteen-year-old daughter of his godparents, an illustration of the close bonds between the Spanish families of Yucatán. Similarly, his three sisters married three brothers of the Cámara y Valdes family. Lorenzo's union was almost certainly a traditional arranged marriage, given the age of the couple and the lack of the bridegroom's financial means. On April 11, 1809, Lorenzo became the father of a daughter, María Manuela; within two years Teresa Josefa bore a second daughter, who died as an infant, and on August 26, 1813, she presented Lorenzo with a son, Manuel Lorenzo, Jr. This young man would accompany his father to Texas and serve at the Battle of San Jacinto.

No more children were born to this union in part because of Lorenzo's political activities that led to his incarceration from 1814 to 1817. Teresa Josefa and the children lived with relatives during those years. Because she was not mentioned again until her death in 1831, she may have been in poor health or reluctant to leave Yucatán and follow Lorenzo to

Mexico City and beyond. In any event, they seem to have been estranged by the 1820s.

These were heady times for young intellectuals in the Spanish colonies of the Western Hemisphere. Zavala's birth, for example, coincided with the adoption of the United States Constitution and the beginning of the French Revolution. Restless criollos in Mexico, Venezuela, and Buenos Aires managed to secure smuggled copies of Abbé Raynal's attack detailing European errors in America, Montesquieu's satires on royalty and high churchmen, Voltaire's denunciation of the privileged, and best of all, Rousseau's essays about the worth of the individual and the idea that government should be based on the consent of the governed. Thomas Jefferson's words, "When in the course of human events it becomes necessary...to dissolve the political bands..." were particularly inspirational for ambitious criollos. Spaniards born in the New World could aspire no higher than mid-level positions in government, the military, or the church, the only three avenues to success in Spanish society. The highest offices were awarded to gachupines, peninsular Spaniards from Europe.

Ultimately, however, it was Napoleon Bonaparte who caused the criollos to revolt in 1808 when he imprisoned King Ferdinand VII and installed his own brother, Joseph, on the Spanish throne.

Spaniards on the continent and in the colonies, mostly sound royalists, renounced the foreign usurper by declaring themselves loyal only to the incarcerated king. In 1810 wealthy criollo members of the cabildos (city governments) from Buenos Aires to Bogotá rebelled, but the focus of their anger was the local peninsular Spaniards, not the monarchy itself.

Mexico's rebellion that same year was different. While the criollo intellectuals discussed and argued among themselves, the parish priest at Dolores, a small village northwest of the capital, set off the revolution. Father Miguel Hidalgo, banished to the village by the Inquisition for his liberal political beliefs, found friends in nearby Querétaro. Convinced that the Spanish authorities had discovered their plotting, on September 16, 1810, he precipitously issued his rallying call. "Long live our Lady of Guadalupe, down with bad government, death to the Spaniards," were the words that started a ragged army of thousands, mostly poor Indians, toward the cities. Hidalgo was captured and executed on July 31, 1811, but the movement continued as guerrilla warfare until 1814 when King Ferdinand VII returned to the throne after the defeat of Napoleon.

Against this background, Zavala and fellow liberals debated their course in isolated, independent Yucatán. By 1810 they met weekly to discuss the ideas found in the smuggled books of Locke, Voltaire, Rousseau, and others. Because there were no newspapers in Yucatán, Zavala wrote articles critical of the Spanish officials, both civil and clerical, and circulated them in manuscript form or read them at gatherings. The Inquisition, now more concerned with maintaining the status quo and burning inflammatory literature than eliminating heretics, ordered Zavala to appear in Mexico City. From distant Mérida, Zavala denied its jurisdiction over political matters. Fortunately for him, time and distance were on his side and the charges against him lapsed.

In Spain leaders called a meeting of a national *Cortes* in 1810. This legislative body had been summoned occasionally in the past by kings as a way to pit the church, the nobles, and the municipalities against each other in order to secure the royal wishes. Delegates, including one from Yucatán, met in unoccupied Cádiz on the southwest coast of Spain, not far from Gibraltar. In 1812, they adopted a reform constitution calling for a limited monarchy; the colonies were invited to send representatives to future meetings. These deputies were to be chosen indirectly in each community by a three-layer system of electors. At the local level, most adult male residents, except blacks, could cast an oral vote for a leading citizen. This was a radical first step toward representative government.

When word reached Mérida about the new constitution, Zavala and his associates formed a new Society of San Juan. Originally organized by the chaplain of the Hermitage of San Juan Bautista to improve the conditions of the Indians, the *sanjuanistas* now became political. They accepted the principles of reform and spread the ideas in opposition to the local *serviles*, those conservatives who continued to support the king, the church, and the old regime.

The *sanjuanista* movement spread to other towns in Yucatán and in early 1813 the group, with the aid of the Mérida municipal council, brought a printing press to the capital city. This first press in Yucatán was now possible because the Constitution of 1812 allowed freedom of expression.

In April 1813, Zavala became the first editor and principal contributor to *El Aristarco Universal (The Universal Critic)*. He also founded and edited *El Redacter Meridiano (The Mérida Compiler)* and *El Filósofo Meridiano (The Mérida Philosopher)* during the next year. These short-lived publications established his lifelong interest in newspapers by demonstrating firsthand the power of the press to shape public opinion.

The Mérida *sanjuanistas*, homogeneous to a degree, divided over some local issues. The chaplain wanted to concentrate on reforms to help the Indians, while Zavala and others were more interested in wider political and religious freedom. This quarrel spread to the Seminario Conciliar, where students revolted. The *sanjuanistas* seized the opportunity to influence local youths by immediately opening their own college known as the House of Studies. It became so popular that it emptied classrooms at the seminary. Zavala and several friends taught classes that included Latin and Spanish grammar, philosophy, and the concepts of constitutional law.

Zavala's anticlericalism increased in 1814 when the captain-general of Yucatán granted the clergy the right to collect tithes from the Indians. Zavala denounced the tax in his newspaper, and even some serviles were angry over this religious levy on the abjectly poor: one, Juan José Duarte, author and member of the provincial assembly, called for a meeting to consider ways to indemnify the clergy if they would relinquish the tithe. He wanted Zavala and three other *sanjuanistas* to attend, but churchmen refused to include the radical reformers. Zavala retained sympathy for the Indians and later, as governor of the State of Mexico, tried to provide land for Indian villages.

Meanwhile, Zavala held a variety of appointed and elected local offices, some of which paid stipends. Under the new constitution, Zavala's neighbors chose him an elector during the parish voting. He then attended the district meeting where he cast a ballot for an elector to select Yucatán's deputies to the *Cortes*. He also became secretary to the *ayuntamiento*, a popularly elected city council; his duties were writing letters and reports. This was a paid position that placed him among the best men of the city. In 1813 the *Cortes* had created a censorship board to prevent the dissemination of inflammatory material against the Constitution of 1812, a somewhat ironic imitation of the Inquisition. This body in turn named members to provincial boards, and in Yucatán Zavala was named along with his mentor, Pablo Moreno, and other *sanjuanistas*. The crowning achievement, however, was his election in March 1814 as one of Yucatán's deputies for the next session of the *Cortes*. Unfortunately, Zavala's anticipated trip to Europe was crushed when Napoleon abdicated in April and King Ferdinand VII returned to the Spanish throne in May.

The king immediately restored his absolute monarchy by abolishing the *Cortes* and its Constitution of 1812. In Mérida reaction was swift and the reform-minded *sanjuanistas* were targets for reprisal. Three of Zavala's associates were sent to the local prison, but a harsher fate awaited the major ringleaders. Zavala, José Matías Quintana (the elderly father of Zavala's classmate, Andrés Quintana Roo), and Francisco Bates were arrested at their homes late at night on July 26, 1814, tried before the captain-general, Artazo y Barral, and threatened with a firing squad. Before dawn the three were on their way to the port of Sisal where a boat took them to San Juan de Ulúa, the notorious island prison in the harbor at Veracruz.

This involuntary journey was Zavala's first trip out of Yucatán. Not quite twenty-six years old, he endured dark and damp cells, some of which flooded during high tides, and poor food. Given the custom of the day, he was probably able to contract for better rations and nicer quarters.

Books circulated through the prison, and over the next three years Zavala taught himself English and read medical books. Just as important for his future, he learned the secrets of freemasonry from fellow political prisoners. The order of Freemasons had entered Spain from France in the early 1700s, brought by advisors to the Bourbon kings. Its members adopted and spread the ideas of the Enlightenment: all men had inalienable rights; government, subject to the will of the people, should protect those rights; government should be free from religious institutions. Masons encouraged vigorous criticism and thus became targets for both the reactionaries and the Roman Catholic Church. Seemingly, freemasonry had not penetrated Yucatán before 1814, but Zavala would carry these tenets for the rest of his life.

Sometime in 1817, Zavala, Quintana, and Bates were released from the old fortress. Zavala remained briefly in Veracruz where he met with men who wanted independence from Spain but were not yet in favor of a republic. He returned to Mérida a hero and began to practice medicine to support his family. As a physician, Zavala was welcome in the homes of the rich and the powerful, thereby establishing important contacts.

Constantly under surveillance by the Spanish authorities,

Zavala and friends secretly organized the first Masonic lodge in Yucatán. The Reunión a la Virtud Lodge #9 received its charter from the Louisiana Grand Lodge in 1817. In spite of the Masons' liberal political philosophy, a few former serviles were initiated.

In January 1820, a liberal revolt in Spain forced Ferdinand VII to restore the Constitution of 1812. Word reached Yucatán by early May, and Zavala and others worried that the captain-general might suppress it on the peninsula. To force the issue, Zavala and a military friend secretly left Mérida for Campeche to urge Masons in the old port to rally public support for the constitution. A meeting there on May 9 endorsed the restoration of the constitutional monarchy, and the captain-general finally promulgated the new order.

Zavala had already reorganized the *sanjuanistas* with some of his Masonic brothers, but the membership split into factions when the Constitution of 1812 was restored. Some supported the Spanish constitutional monarchy while others dreamed of an independent Mexico with its own limited monarchy. Those favoring a republic were a radical minority. Zavala remained cautiously neutral and told his associates: "If the king will protect our rights we will obey him, but if he will not, then we must secure our independence."

Zavala was apparently ready for an independent Mexico if the king was uncooperative, but he probably was not ready for a republic. Few criollos were. A 1990 study of Agustín Iturbide's empire by Timothy E. Anna offers convincing arguments that through 1822 there was no talk about a republic. Zavala, for example, wrote in his *Ensayo Histórico* that while there were republicans in the Mexican Congress that year, none called for a republic. Most Mexicans wanted the status quo: a country with an established church and the traditional military and clerical privileges. The word "republic" projected the frightening image of the French Revolution and the experiment with a republic in the 1790s; only a few Mexicans knew much about the North American republic.

During the summer and fall of 1820, Zavala was a member and secretary of Yucatán's provincial assembly. In August his neighbors nominated him as one of five Yucatán deputies to the *Cortes* scheduled to meet at Madrid in March. Electors at the subsequent district meeting and the provincial election confirmed the choice.

Events in Mérida soon convinced Zavala that independence was the only way to eliminate what he viewed as arrogant and arbitrary behavior by Yucatán's political chief and the new captain-general, both appointive positions under Spanish law. These two Spanish officials, of course, tried to suppress anyone advocating independence. The political chief dissolved both the Mérida *ayuntamiento* and the provincial assembly in October, while the captain-general ordered the arrest of troublesome priests and officials, including Zavala.

The troops seized Zavala while he was visiting at the Hermitage of San Juan Bautista. As an elected deputy to the *Cortes*, he claimed immunity from political arrest. Six hours later the captain-general released Zavala after the he agreed to sail immediately for Spain.

Zavala bid his family good-bye and sailed for Havana. There on October 26, he published a pamphlet denouncing his recent arrest as despotism. He soon left Havana for Madrid where he arrived in January 1821. Zavala and a fellow Yucatán deputy presented their credentials on February 23, and in spite of protests about illegal voting, they were seated the next day. He was named to several committees and immediately filed a report detailing his trouble with the Mérida authorities, claiming their actions violated the 1812 Constitution. He asked that deputies be given immunity from arbitrary arrest. Following his presentation, the captain-general's brothers offered evidence against Zavala to exonerate their kinsman. The matter was sent to the proper committee for study, always the solution for thorny issues.

Deputies from other Spanish colonies also had complaints

about arbitrary officials but the European-dominated *Cortes* showed little interest. The colonial deputies held meetings in June to discuss their frustrations, and Zavala and two others were asked to draft documents clarifying the rights of elected delegates. The final report, a composite, included a request that the Madrid parliament create three autonomous congresses for the Western Hemisphere: one in Mexico, another in northern South America, and the third in Buenos Aires. Each division would have its own executive appointed by the king. The Europeans, however, rejected the plan as beyond the constitutional power of the *Cortes*, while the colonial deputies complained they were unable to represent the interests of their constituents. However, Zavala wrote later that the proposal was basically propaganda for use at home to foster independence.

Before the end of the legislative session, word reached the *Cortes* about the *Plan de Iguala* adopted by a coalition of diverse Mexican interests on February 2, 1821. This first step toward Mexican independence occurred when General Agustín de Iturbide, a former criollo officer in the Spanish army, defected and forged a union with General Vicente Guerrero, the major rebel leader in the south. The *Plan de Iguala* made three guarantees to unite all factions: first, *religion*—the establishment of the Roman Catholic Church; second, *independence*—from Spain with a constitutional monarch; and third, *equality*—of citizenship for criollos and European Spaniards who accepted the terms. This uneasy coalition of monarchists and republicans made pragmatic political compromises in order to achieve their common goal: separation from Spanish control. Their united army marched under the tricolor banner of red, white, and green.

The newly arrived Spanish viceroy, O'Donoju, now called the captain-general and superior political chief, signed the Treaty of Córdova based on Iturbide's plan on August 24, 1821. Aware that most of the country including the army had endorsed the plan, he bowed to the superior force and, without authorization from his government, acknowledged Mexico's independence. He defended his action because the plan and the treaty both called for a Spanish Bourbon prince to sit on the Mexican throne. Thus, he claimed, he had saved the large and rich kingdom of Mexico for the Spanish monarchy.

Iturbide, as the acknowledged head of the temporary government, led the Army of the Three Guarantees into Mexico City in September. At this same time, leaders in Mérida met and declared the peninsula independent of Spain, though they retained the Spanish captain-general. Two months later Yucatán joined the Mexican empire.

During the summer adjournment of the *Cortes*, Zavala, discouraged by the lack of progress in Madrid and aware of Mexican independence, applied for permission to return home. Not waiting for approval from the members who would convene on September 22, he went to France, perhaps intending to sail from the busy port of Bordeaux. For some reason, he delayed and remained in France until the end of the year.

For a man yet to see Mexico City, being in Europe was exciting; no doubt he wanted to see as much of it as he could with limited means. Before September 15 he was in Paris, perhaps involved with plotters there who wanted to place a descendant of the Aztec monarch, Moctezuma, on the Mexican throne. There were a number of Mexicans living in both Spain and France, and if a man was clever and personable, he might solicit invitations to visit while exchanging opinions about politics. Zavala also may have practiced medicine to help cover his expenses.

He finally sailed from Bordeaux and arrived in New Orleans on December 24. This was his first visit to the United States, albeit in one of its most cosmopolitan cities. The Crescent City had long been a haven for Mexican refugees, and Zavala probably made contacts before sailing for

Yucatán. He arrived home in early 1822, ready to take a role in Mexican politics now that Yucatán had joined the other former provinces of the Viceroyalty of New Spain.

CHAPTER 3

Zavala and the Republic of Mexico, 1822-1830

SOON AFTER he arrived in Mérida, Zavala was elected a deputy to the constituent congress meeting in Mexico City. He sent letters to the various Yucatán town councils asking what kind of government they preferred: a republic or a monarchy? If the latter, from which royal family should a king be chosen? Did they want religious toleration?

He later recalled, "I . . . [did] not know which was the best suited to a new nation which had neither republican habits, nor monarchial elements. Everything would be trials or experiments until a form . . . was discovered." His questions, framed in innocence and a sincere desire for guidance, made the members of the *ayuntamientos* uneasy. Nothing in their Spanish heritage prepared them for the give-and-take representation Zavala offered.

Zavala sailed to Veracruz where the Spanish army still occupied the fortress of San Juan de Ulúa, his former prison, and controlled shipping in the harbor. Once ashore, the Yucatán deputy could choose between a coach, an enclosed litter suspended between two mules, or horseback to travel the mountainous route to Mexico City. The road climbed forty-six hundred feet in the first seventy miles, from the tropical sand hills near Veracruz to a more pleasant climate at Jalapa; then it continued upward to Puebla and Mexico City, both over seven thousand feet in elevation. The entire journey, less than three hundred miles, could be made in eleven days but it often took longer.

Zavala took his oath of office on March 30, 1822, and was soon assigned to several committees including two of immediate interest to him: colonization and finance. Nothing in his education seemed to have prepared him for the latter, but like Alexander Hamilton in the United States, he understood that the new nation had to seek foreign loans and establish credit by paying its debts. This meant taxation and paper money, both unpopular with most people.

The colonization committee discussed at length whether or not to allow foreigners, particularly Anglo American cotton producers, to settle in Texas as a way for economic development of the remote frontier. Zavala, who could understand English, met with several United States citizens who, for their own reasons, wanted empresario contracts to settle Anglo American families in Texas. Among the applicants were Stephen F. Austin, General James Wilkinson, Benjamin Rush Milam, and agents for some Tennessee speculators. From these men, Zavala learned about Texas' superior advantages in location, terrain, and fertile soil. The economic potential for successful colonizers intrigued the Yucatecan, and the seed was planted for his future speculation in Texas land.

Austin had an advantage over the others because he had inherited a colonization contract from his father. The Austin contract to settle three hundred Anglo families along the lower Brazos and Colorado rivers in Texas had been issued on

January 17, 1821, by the Spanish commandant general at Monterrey. This official held supreme civil and military jurisdiction over Texas and adjacent provinces, and in sharp contrast with Spain's previous policy forbidding the entrance of foreigners, he authorized the Austin contract under the reinstated Constitution of 1812. Moses Austin died shortly after receiving the grant, which forced the son to travel to San Antonio in August 1821 to confirm the inherited contract with the Spanish governor. On his return to Louisiana, he explored the Texas coast for the best location for his colony.

When empresario Austin returned to Texas to begin settlement in early 1822, Mexican independence had been achieved. Austin had to go to Mexico City to have the contract approved by the new government. His meetings with Zavala and other members of the colonization committee gave him hope for quick approval, but the installation of General Agustín de Iturbide as emperor in May would delay final action for a year.

Zavala had been in Mexico City less than two months when, on the night of May 18, the army and a mob demanded Iturbide be made emperor rather than accept a European prince. Since entering Mexico City in September, Iturbide had ruled the new nation as president of the ad interim regency and was also commander-in-chief of the army.

Historians do not agree why Iturbide became emperor at this time. Some modern scholars believe that his coronation occurred because reformers in congress were about to pass a law prohibiting military commanders from holding high civil office. Zavala may have been one of those reformers. In *Porvenir de México ó Juicio sobre Su Estado Político en 1821 y 1851,* author Luis Gonzaga Cuevas, without offering evidence, claimed that Zavala, his old friend, Andrés Quintana Roo, then subsecretary of state, and idealist Valentín Gómez Farías helped make Iturbide emperor. Zavala said later that he was neutral and that he offered sanctuary to Iturbide's enemies the night the mob ran through the capital.

The next day congress voted to accept the emperor if he would "pledge himself . . . to obey the constitution, laws, orders, and decrees which emanate from the sovereign Mexican Congress." Zavala's name was not on the official record when seventy-seven unidentified deputies, less than half, voted for the emperor; five more wanted the issue referred to the provinces. Many deputies were absent. In spite of some congressional reluctance to endorse the empire, Zavala believed that a plebiscite of the provinces would have resulted in a free election of Iturbide. Over the next ten months of the transitory empire, Zavala maintained a guarded relationship with the emperor.

Zavala worked hard to complete the colonization committee's report during June and July. It was difficult to gain consensus for a law pleasing to Anglo supplicants and addressing the xenophobia of conservatives. Fear of encroachment from the United States was very real for those who recalled how Spain had lost Baton Rouge and Mobile to the United States between 1811 and 1813. Another concern was whether or not slavery-for-life as it existed in the United States would be permitted in Texas or if some sort of time limit should be imposed. Zavala defended the report as written, and when it was sent back for revision on July 23, he asked permission to resign from the committee, a request that was refused.

Amid these arguments, the emperor ordered fifteen deputies arrested on August 26, charging them with conspiracy to overthrow the government. Congress was so upset by the events that a month passed before normal business resumed. Zavala argued on August 29 that Iturbide had violated the power of the executive as described in the Spanish Constitution of 1812, the temporary basis of Mexican government. While the executive could arrest those who threatened public security, he had to deliver them to a court within forty-eight hours, which Iturbide had not done. Zavala thought that congress should dissolve itself because it was vulnerable to dismissal or even arrest. The following day Zavala and three others worked on a manifesto defending the conduct of the deputies to be given to the public should the emperor dissolve congress.

One month later, on September 25, 1822, frustrated with inaction, Zavala denounced congress. Calling it paralyzed by feuds and jealousies, he listed its faults: from the first, members had disregarded basic rules by not having a quorum and by giving executive power to the regency without the consent of the people; Congress had ignored the legislative limits in the 1812 Spanish constitution and also refused to divide itself into two houses; Congress ignored pressing financial problems, and many deputies had to retire because of the lack of salaries. Zavala may have been speaking about his own financial condition.

Zavala, once for a constitutional monarchy, now moved toward republicanism. Soon critics called him a radical republican and the head of the liberal "Jacobin" party, a reference to Robespierre's role through the Reign of Terror during the French Revolution. The Yucatecan called for the dissolution of the current unicameral legislature and the election of a bicameral Congress with the lower house based on population, not an arbitrary number. His criticism and suggestions created a sensation, and tradition-minded delegates denounced Zavala. He answered his critics in a pamphlet that outlined reforms resembling the powers held by the United States Congress. He called for more checks and balances on executive and legislative powers. A bicameral Congress, he said, would prevent congressional tyranny; likewise, an executive veto power would provide an option short of arresting or dismissing members of Congress.

The emperor seized this opportunity for reform and convened a panel of advisors including deputies, generals, and other officials to discuss the issues. Iturbide agreed that Congress should be reduced to seventy members. Congress refused at first but quickly complied on October 31 when Iturbide sent a general with an order to adjourn within the hour. The emperor then named a forty-five-member *junta nacional instituyente* of former deputies including Zavala to begin work immediately on the constitution, certain laws, and the formation of a new Congress.

The *junta* was organized on November 2, and Zavala was named to four committees: finance, colonization, and two others concerned with the writing and publication of the acts of the *junta*. The colonization law received immediate attention. Zavala and four others who had earlier struggled with the bill revised the wording to make it acceptable to critics who feared foreign colonists. The document went to Iturbide on the last day of the year and he signed it January 4, 1823. Austin's contract in Texas was the only empresario grant made under this colonization law because of the demise of the empire. Subsequent empresario contracts in Texas were issued by the state government.

By the close of 1822, Zavala, still the Jacobin, questioned the legitimacy of the *junta* on grounds that it was not representative of the nation. In January he openly challenged a constitution Iturbide intended to impose on the nation in lieu of calling a new constitutional convention. Conservatives called Zavala a chameleon and said they were shocked by the ease with which he changed opinions. Zavala defended himself for attacking the constituent Congress and for first supporting, then challenging the empire by explaining that his were the acts of a man seeking what was best for his country given the changing times. These statements reveal the pragmatic Zavala, a man struggling for reform but a realist.

Zavala was not alone in criticizing Iturbide's empire. Generals Antonio López de Santa Anna, Guadalupe Victoria, Vicente Guerrero, and many other high-ranking army officers united on February 1, 1823, as "republicans" and demanded a new representative Congress. To appease his critics, Iturbide recalled the old Congress on March 4, but its members, including those sent to prison by the emperor, refused to act until troops loyal to Iturbide were removed from the capital.

Unwilling to use arms to sustain himself in office, Iturbide abdicated on March 19 and left the country in May with his family. Congress named a military triumvirate to act as the executive branch while the new constituent Congress drafted a suitable constitution. Zavala and the others invalidated all legislation passed during the empire—from May 19, 1822, to March 29, 1823. Austin's colonial contract, however, remained in force.

The monarchy was a dead issue, but the country was divided into two political factions. Liberals favored a federalist republic, somewhat like Thomas Jefferson's ideal, with strong states and limited central government, while conservatives wanted the more familiar strong central government they remembered under the Crown and the Roman Catholic Church. The army generals, high churchmen, and the wealthy drifted toward centralism; Zavala, of course, was a federalist.

The new Congress assembled in November 1823 with a federalist majority, and by November 20 a preliminary draft was submitted outlining the new republic. Zavala took an active part in the debates during 1824 and was elected vice president of Congress during August and president the following month. Outvoting the centralists seventy to ten, the federalists issued a constitution for the Republic of Mexico in October 1824.

On the surface it resembled that of the United States by having three branches of government, a bicameral Congress, and a president and vice president elected for four-year terms. The concept of dual federalism was extended to the nineteen states, each having its own elected governor and legislature. In the first election, the state legislatures chose federalist Guadalupe Victoria, a hero of the revolution, as president, and the runner-up, General Nicolás Bravo, another revolutionary leader, as vice president. This clumsy pairing of victor and runner-up, also used by the United States before 1804, led to trouble.

27

Zavala was elected senator from Yucatán and took his seat in December 1824. Named to the financial, constitutional, and judicial committees, he served through 1826. As in the constituent Congress, he was honored by one month's term as vice president of the senate in 1825 and a similar month as president in 1826.

In October 1825, President Guadalupe Victoria offered Zavala the post of minister to Washington, D. C., but he declined, much to the relief of his friend, Joel R. Poinsett, the United States minister to Mexico. Poinsett wrote to Secretary of State Henry Clay that Zavala "is one of the most efficient leaders . . . friendly to the United States . . . and is more useful here than he would be in Washington."

Poinsett, the first United States minister to Mexico, landed at Veracruz in May 1825 and was received officially in the capital in June. Previously he had served in South America as a consul and had visited Mexico in 1822, when he and Zavala began their lifelong friendship. The two were similar in intellectual curiosity. A native of South Carolina, wealthy, and ten years older than Zavala, Poinsett was educated in Great Britain. He studied medicine and the law, liked neither, and instead, traveled for a decade through Europe. With a keen ear for languages, he became knowledgeable about European cultures; from 1811 to 1815 he served as United States agent and consul in Argentina, Chile, and Peru. When he returned home to South Carolina, his friends elected him to the state legislature and then to the United States Congress. Thus he and Zavala had many interests in common.

Within three months of Poinsett's arrival in Mexico City, a number of Masons asked him to secure York Rite charters from the United States to establish new Mexican lodges. The Scottish Rite order had been in Mexico for a number of years and was the lodge of conservative centralists and of the British minister to Mexico. The republican federalists, including President Guadalupe Victoria and Zavala, were no longer comfortable in the Scottish Rite order. Moreover, the British minister used his Scottish Rite membership as a tool to influence the conservative centralists. Poinsett, instructed by his government to encourage democracy and ties with the United States, quickly secured York Rite charters for the new lodges. Before long, however, the centralists accused him of taking part in Mexican politics.

The two fraternal orders became the two political parties between 1825 and 1828. The new *yorkinos* became so popular that some Scottish Rite lodges (*escoceses*) transferred their entire membership and records to the new organization. The proliferation of secret lodges made some leaders uneasy— political intrigue and even revolution might be nurtured in clandestine meetings of the fraternal lodges. Even Senator Zavala, seemingly for political reasons, supported bills in the senate that urged restrictions against secret societies, although he held offices in several York Rite lodges. The *yorkinos* continued to grow as a political force, determined to defeat the *escoceses* whose members tended to be the elite: the landed wealthy, the bureaucracy, many generals, high churchmen, and former monarchists.

Zavala grew weary of his legislative role by 1826 and yearned for a position of direct leadership. His new goal was the governorship of the State of Mexico. He had introduced the bill in November 1824 that carved a federal district for Mexico City out of the center of the state. The district's boundary was a ten-mile-wide circle stretching out from the main plaza. Critics said Zavala had planned the removal of the federal capital from the State of Mexico so that he would have only the unlettered farmers to govern.

In order to participate politically in the rich, fertile state, he had to own land or have an established residence. Zavala lacked the personal fortune to acquire such property. However, a wealthy friend and supporter of the federalist cause, Doña María Mercedes Trebuest y Casasola, the Countess of Miravalle (the seventh generation to hold the Spanish title), arranged for him to acquire a country house at

San Agustín de las Cuevas "Tlalpam". A little over ten miles south of Mexico City on the road to Cuernavaca, San Agustín was once a popular rural retreat for the nobility and rich merchants from the city. The scattered houses and beautiful gardens were abandoned during the war for independence, and in 1826 the settlement remained largely unpopulated except during its annual three-day fair in May.

Zavala took part in the San Agustín elections on September 6, 1826, and was chosen an elector to attend the state convention at Toluca where state and national legislators would be chosen. His enemies challenged his election and a substitute was named; nevertheless, Zavala arrived in Toluca on September 25 and served as secretary of the meeting.

Besides his personal political ambitions, Zavala and his fellow *yorkinos* wanted to strengthen the party in the important state surrounding the federal district. Zavala's enemies claimed that he bought clothing for poorly clad electors, used government troops to bolster the party's image, and packed the galleries with bullies who intimidated inexperienced electors. Zavala was like a Roman tribune, said one critic, adding that his scandalous conduct was reminiscent of turbulent Rome under Gracchus. Zavala probably did not mind the comparison to the Roman who urged land reforms in favor of the peasants.

Zavala's ambition for the governorship was fulfilled within six months. The incumbent governor unexpectedly resigned on March 7, 1827, and the next day the legislature began balloting for a successor. Zavala received eleven votes to five for General Vicente Guerrero, the former freedom fighter and also a *yorkino*. Five days later Zavala took office and began a sweeping program of public improvement for roads, schools, and libraries; he used funds hoarded by his predecessors.

One of his first goals was to move the state capital from Texcoco, northeast of Mexico City, to Toluca on the west. The legislature refused but approved relocating the seat of state government to San Agustín near Zavala's residence. Five months later, in an effort to restore Mexico's ancient heritage, the deputies gave San Agustín the old name of Tlalpam. Zavala's first choice, beautiful Toluca, once the center of the Toltec empire, finally became the capital in 1830.

The *yorkinos* found good reason to attack the Scottish Rite order in 1827 when a Spanish priest tried to recruit several military leaders among the *escoceses* to restore Spanish sovereignty in Mexico. Zavala condemned both parties: the Scottish Rite for fomenting uprisings in order to attack Guadalupe Victoria's administration and the *yorkinos* for arousing the public by demanding the expulsion of all Spaniards. Zavala once again followed his own conscience and called for reason, but found it a "weak voice . . . against the torrent of factions." The York Rite Grand Lodge censured him for supporting the Spaniards, while the *gachupines*, the European-born Spaniards, opposed everything he did. In retrospect, Zavala believed the Spanish issue was the beginning of his political troubles.

The national Congress ordered the removal of all Spaniards from office in May 1827, and the legislature of the State of Mexico debated the issue in August. Governor Zavala received daily reports, most fictitious, that Spaniards in the state were gathering arms to destroy the government. He was reluctant to remove the Spaniards because it would have a negative economic effect: departing Spaniards would remove their investments, which would injure trade and commerce.

Zavala had some notable successes in the field of education while he was governor. The creation and funding of a state library were well underway. Books he had personally ordered from Europe were due to arrive to be shelved in the state capital; some books would be located elsewhere in the state at a later date. He opened a public, rather than church-controlled, college by converting the former Colegio Seminario to a public institution. The legislature failed to fund the undertaking in September 1827, but, staffed in part with volunteers, the school nevertheless offered classes in French, Latin, Castillian grammar; civil, canon, and public law; philosophy; and political economy. By the following spring, the state provided funds and the Literary Institute opened.

Zavala's first English-speaking biographer, Raymond Estep, views Zavala as the father of the agrarian movement in Mexico. The Yucatecan, echoing Thomas Jefferson, believed that the national economy should be based on the development of agriculture rather than industry as proposed by Lucas Alamán, a wealthy, well-educated, conservative contemporary. As governor, Zavala divided land that had been in litigation for years to provide land to more than forty Indian villages in the valley of Toluca. Zavala firmly believed that Indians should have arable land instead of being forced to work for others as peons forever in debt. To redistribute the wealth and provide for Indian lands, Zavala proposed to tax absentee landlords: ten percent on the land of those who resided outside of Mexico and a smaller levy on landowners residing in another Mexican state. The proceeds would be given to the landless to buy farms. While there was little progress, the seeds for future reforms were planted in 1827. In April 1828, these seeds led to opposition and bloodshed.

Meanwhile national politics simmered, not only over the issue of expelling the Spaniards, but also about the political influence being exerted by the ministers representing Great Britain and the United States and their membership in the Masonic orders. Both nations sought trade advantages. H. G. Ward, the British minister, was a polished diplomat who lavishly entertained the "right" people and won the support of conservative centralists. His efforts resulted in a trade treaty for Great Britain in 1825. Meanwhile, Poinsett, an ardent republican closely involved with the federalist *yorkinos* and a personal friend of Zavala, was unable to secure an agreement for the United States until 1828, and even then the Mexican Congress failed to act.

The aristocratic party launched an attack against Poinsett in 1827 and demanded his recall because he participated in Mexican politics. During the summer Zavala defended his South Carolina friend and warned *yorkinos* that Poinsett's resignation would be a blow to the federalist cause. The Yucatecan again defended the maligned minister in January 1828 by publishing a pamphlet supporting Poinsett's actions in Mexico and detailing his earlier aid to republicans in Chile. This defense followed the Montaño affair.

In December 1827, Manuel Montaño, in a move to overthrow President Guadalupe Victoria, demanded the recall of Poinsett, the expulsion of the Spaniards (actually a red herring), the elimination of secret orders, and the removal of moderate Manuel Gómez Pedraza as secretary of war. It was a Scottish Rite plot financed in part by the Spaniards. General Vicente Guerrero, a federalist, moved quickly to suppress the movement in January. His three thousand troops defeated a centralist army led by General Nicolás Bravo, the vice president. The federalists triumphed and sent the centralist leaders into exile. Zavala blamed the affair on the reactionary centralist faction that did not understand that the public wanted the new political and economic opportunities offered by the federalist *yorkinos*.

Zavala continued to use newspapers to disseminate his political views. When the *Aguila Mexicana* began publishing in Mexico City in 1823, he had contributed articles and become well known as a journalist. When the *yorkinos* became a political party and established the *Correo de la Federación Mexicana* in 1826, Zavala was a regular contributor. On June 4, 1828, he and Cornelius C. Sebring, a South Carolina adventurer and friend of Poinsett, bought the press and the newspaper. It was more than a political interest—their five-year contract allowed each to draw an annual salary of 2,000 pesos and divide all profits. Without a wealthy family or a comfortable inheritance like some of his colleagues, Zavala always needed income.

It was for this reason that Zavala applied for an empresario contract to settle 500 families in Texas in April 1828. Empresarios received no money from the colonists, but the government allowed them about 23,000 acres for every 100 families they settled, a potential of 115,000 acres that perhaps could be sold for fifty cents per acre, or around $57,000. There were rumors that the United States might acquire eastern Texas, and the land granted to Zavala was a fifty-two-mile-wide strip bordering the west bank of the Sabine River from the well-traveled Old Spanish Road to Nacogdoches, then south to the Gulf, and a twenty-six-mile-wide strip along the coast to Galveston Bay. Even though he was a native Mexican, unlike many of the other empresarios, a prominent public figure, and a personal friend of José María Viesca, the governor of the state of Coahuila-Texas (the two sparsely populated provinces had been joined in 1824), final approval by the national government was delayed until February 1829 because of politics. Even before the contract was issued, Zavala named Thomas R. Luckett his agent in the United States to explore the possibility of selling the contract. Although such a sale subverted the intent of the national and state colonization laws, Zavala was not the only Mexican citizen willing to profit from Texas lands should opportunity arise. Pragmatic men recognized and welcomed economic enterprise and the exploitation of natural resources.

As the second presidential election drew near in 1828, both the Scottish Rite and York Rite lodges vied for the office. The Constitution of 1824 denied a second term to the incumbent, thereby opening the gates for the ambitious. The York Rite Grand Lodge unanimously supported Vicente Guerrero for president. He was master of the Grand Lodge, a hero of the War for Independence, and the recent victor in the Montaño uprising. The members split between Zavala and José Ignacio Esteva for vice president; to avoid controversy, they decided to support Anastasio Bustamante. While most *yorkinos* supported these candidates, several *ayuntamientos* in Zavala's state endorsed a slate of Guerrero and Zavala.

The *escoceses* were handicapped by the recent Montaño affair because their favored candidate, Nicolás Bravo, had been exiled. The lodge turned to fellow member Manuel Gómez Pedraza, a moderate who was serving in President Guadalupe Victoria's cabinet. The campaign became vicious when newspapers indulged in slander and defamation of character. Secrets in the private lives of the candidates were exploited as well as perceived errors in judgment during past public service. The excesses of this campaign and schisms within both Scottish Rite and York Rite lodges signaled the end of the Masonic brotherhoods as political parties. Hereafter, the fight was between conservative centralism and liberal federalism.

The election of 1828 and the unrest that followed for the next four years set a precedent for violence in future campaigns. Voting for the president and vice president was indirect; state legislatures polled their members on September 1 with the majority providing the state's one vote. Gómez Pedraza, supported by many "impartials" who were outraged by the campaign, won the electoral votes of eleven legislatures. Guerrero secured only nine. Zavala deplored the indirect method; he believed that if the people had been able to vote directly, Guerrero would have won. Guerrero's followers refused to abide by the vote, which they suspected had been manipulated, and they considered ways to prevent Gómez Pedraza from assuming office in 1829.

General Antonio López de Santa Anna, commandant at Veracruz, ever sensitive to opportunity, voiced his opposition early in September. Zavala, lining up federalist support, wrote to the "Hercules" of Veracruz praising his action. Lame-duck President Guadalupe Victoria, even though a federalist, removed Santa Anna from his command, but the ambitious *caudillo* retaliated by leading eight hundred men from his home near Jalapa to occupy the fortress at Perote. On

September 11 Santa Anna publicly denied the legitimacy of Gómez Pedraza's election and promised to fight until Guerrero was seated. Congress outlawed the fiery officer, and administration troops surrounded Perote. Santa Anna was prevented from further action, but popular discontent only increased.

Governor Zavala, still attached to the Guerrero candidacy, tried to remain publicly neutral and to effect a compromise to avoid the use of arms. However, Gómez Pedraza, the president-elect, was suspicious and accused Zavala of complicity in revolutionary plotting.

Government troops arrived in Tlalpam to arrest Zavala. Facing the dilemma of submitting or becoming a fugitive, the Yucatecan fled to the safety of friends on October 6. In retaliation, the government seized his property and had it inventoried for sale.

Zavala remained hidden in the hills of his state until the end of the month when he quietly slipped into Mexico City, where he remained secluded while federalists laid plans for a coup. Zavala's associates seized the old military barracks and prison of the Acordada on November 30; for the next four days, the fugitive directed violence that resulted in the sacking of the marketplace owned by Spanish merchants and the execution of a supporter of Gómez Pedraza. Zavala's leadership in this uprising, known as the Cuartelazo de la Acordada, severely damaged his reputation as a liberal reformer with Mexican historians.

Zavala negotiated an armistice with lame-duck President Guadalupe Victoria on December 4, resulting in a settlement four days later. The president removed Gómez Pedraza as secretary of war in his cabinet, while Zavala allowed the hapless man to flee the country. The federalist president then named Vicente Guerrero to the vacated cabinet post, thereby giving him stature, and left him the obvious president-elect.

The *escoceses*, having lost their presidential candidate, decided to drive a wedge between the *yorkino* leaders: Zavala,

Guerrero, and Santa Anna. They focused on Zavala, accusing him of wanting to become dictator. President-elect Guerrero ignored the rumors and offered Zavala a range of appointments, out of which he chose secretary of the treasury and, with the aid of soon-to-be-replaced President Guadalupe Victoria, also resumed his governorship before the end of the year.

President Guerrero was installed in April 1829, with the legitimately elected Anastasio Bustamante as vice president. On April 18, Zavala took his oath in the cabinet while the state legislature allowed him to continue as governor. His tenure in both would be brief—just under six months.

No man in Mexico had more vision than Zavala for the difficult task of stabilizing and rehabilitating the finances of the nation. When Zavala took charge of the treasury, the country was bankrupt. The various uprisings had consumed government funds, Spanish merchants had moved gold and silver out of the country, the states failed to pay their contributions, and foreign commerce was dead. Neither the army nor the civil servants had been paid for some time. Zavala proposed drastic cuts in spending and new taxes and fees to produce income. As an emergency measure, he limited government creditors to only one-third of the customs house receipts, the only accessible source for specie. The remaining two-thirds were sent to the treasury to cover the most pressing needs. Zavala proposed a variety of license fees and the abandonment of federal responsibility for state debts. Naturally, his program was unpopular, and his enemies quickly seized the moment to blame him for Mexico's economic woes—even accusing him of pilfering. Congress failed to act on these suggestions and instead relied on traditional means—floating loans wherever they could be obtained, usually at usurious rates. Zavala was more successful in persuading Congress to abolish the national tobacco monopoly, a holdover from Spain, that once produced income but now was a hindrance to trade. Congress also established a national income tax. Still short of specie, Zavala proposed a forced loan from the states and asked for a ceiling on civil and military salaries.

During Zavala's fourth month in office, the Spanish landed an army near Tampico intending to reconquer Mexico. Poorly planned and executed, the effort was doomed, but the attack made Santa Anna, now governor of Veracruz, a hero. Within weeks, he forced the Spaniards to surrender. The July invasion gave Secretary of the Treasury Zavala an opportunity to increase income by seizing Spanish property.

All of these desperate attempts to revitalize Mexico's treasury caused pain, and several state legislatures demanded that Zavala be removed from office. Three Yucatecan deputies in Congress accused him of floating the loans and the sale of government tobacco, contrary to the interests of the states; they demanded his indictment. Moreover, Santa Anna, once Zavala's friend, became his enemy when an editorial appeared describing the danger that the "Victor of Tampico" posed to the nation. Zavala had not written the offending article, but Santa Anna was convinced that he had.

Fellow cabinet members shortsightedly failed to support or cooperate with the beleaguered treasury secretary. On October 3 Zavala's enemies within the cabinet asked the legislature of the State of Mexico to revoke the special permission that allowed him to hold both offices. Six days later Zavala resigned from the cabinet and advised President Guerrero to abandon his clique of advisors, saying, "A tempest threatens you within a short time." The beleaguered chief executive, however, could not stop the inevitable coup that soon removed him from office and led to his death before a firing squad.

Intending to resume the governorship full-time, Zavala was denied his office by the legislature on October 15; yet the members allowed him his salary. President Guerrero sent him on a secret mission to Yucatán to quell an uprising—garrisons at Campeche and Mérida had proclaimed a centralist republic on the peninsula in November and removed the governor.

Zavala, however, was not welcome in his native state and was arrested at Sisal on December 5. The military governor released him, but warned that he would be shot if he set foot in Yucatán again. Five days later Zavala returned to Veracruz without even seeing his family.

While Zavala was on his futile mission, Vice President Bustamante, now converted to centralism, began a revolution against President Guerrero on December 4. The president personally led troops to put down the rebellion, but his administration was doomed. While both the president and the vice president were absent from Mexico City, centralists attacked the national palace on December 22. Zavala, visiting there, fled to the mint where he remained briefly before being arrested. The centralists released Zavala on December 29 after he agreed to recognize Bustamante's provisional government. He remained in his home with a centralist guard at the door "to protect him."

Zavala was shaken by his recent humiliation. Faced with a bleak-looking new decade, he considered leaving Mexico. His friend, Joel Poinsett, long the target of the *escoceses*, had been relieved as United States minister and was scheduled to leave Mexico City on January 3, 1830. Zavala wanted to go with him, but his enemies renewed the charges of malfeasance in office while secretary of the treasury. Their accusations and denunciations continued through January, but on February 25, the grand jury found him innocent of the charges. Five days later the senate formally acquitted Zavala.

Again he made plans to leave the city but was detained by another charge—that he had improperly handled contracts. The evidence was scanty and the accusation was solely to delay his departure. He finally left the capital on May 25, 1830, with the help of Lucas Alamán, the new secretary of state in Bustamante's cabinet. Alamán, a centralist and a fellow intellectual, wanted Zavala to leave before he was murdered. Zavala headed for Veracruz and exile in the United States.

4

Political Refugee
and Entrepreneur,
1830-1833

ZAVALA left the capital with mixed emotions and many questions. Was his political career over at the age of forty-one? How long could the centralists remain in power? When and how could the federalists regain control? How could he support himself as a refugee?

His estranged wife and surviving daughter, Manuela, were being cared for by family members and friends while his teenage son, Lorenzo, was in school in New York. Zavala looked forward to seeing his namesake but worried about his personal finances. The recent seizure of his property was a severe financial blow, especially now that he had no income. Only his six-year empresario contract to settle 500 families in Texas offered salvation.

While he had ample funds for the present, he hoped to sell his land in Texas while he was in the United States. Just before Poinsett left Mexico City for the United States, Zavala had made a contract with the former diplomat to find investors for the Texas land.

Fortunately Zavala had good company on his journey to the coast. His friend, Colonel José Antonio Mexía, was returning to his diplomatic post in the United States after a quick trip to Mexico City. The previous November, President Guerrero had named Mexía secretary to the Mexican legation in the United States. Mexía and his family left Mexico at the end of 1830 with the new minister to the United States, José María Tornel. Within four months Tornel sent Mexía back to Mexico City to report a rumored Spanish invasion.

A charming, well-educated opportunist, Mexía, probably a native of Cuba, was twelve years younger than Zavala. He had served in the Mexican struggle for independence and apparently took refuge in the United States where he learned to speak English. In 1822 he was in Texas when Mexican Governor José Félix Trespalacios sent him from San Antonio to Mexico City as interpreter for a group of English-speaking Cherokees who wanted a land grant. Once in the capital, Mexía used his Masonic connections to become an officer in General Nicolás Bravo's army and escorted the deposed Emperor Iturbide to Veracruz. Mexía married Charlotte Walker in Mexico City on August 5, 1823; the spirited young Englishwoman, unlike Zavala's wife, followed her husband from place to place and bore three children by 1829. Through his Masonic and army friends, Mexía secured a series of financially rewarding appointments and, while customs house officer at Tuxpan, managed to accumulate a sizable fortune.

The Mexía family returned to Mexico City in 1827, where the captain became General Guerrero's private secretary. It was at this time that he developed close ties with Zavala, Joel R. Poinsett, and General Santa Anna. During the abortive Spanish invasion in July and August 1829, Mexía, now a colonel, was aide-de-camp to Santa Anna.

Like Zavala, Mexía had interests in Texas. His holdings, however, differed; instead of an empresario grant, he had purchased from friends their rights to unlocated eleven-league tracts (48,708 acres) to be surveyed. These large grants could be acquired by native Mexicans at less than two cents an acre from the state of Coahuila-Texas. Coahuila officials intended to Mexicanize the Texas frontier by encouraging native Mexicans to start settlements and nullify the ever-increasing number of Anglo Americans in Texas. However, most purchasers sold their unlocated grants for immediate profit and usually to Anglo Americans.

Zavala and Mexía, on the advice of friends, had refused a military escort to the coast. Recent assassinations made federalists wary of centralist troops who might be employed by political enemies. Well armed against road bandits, Zavala and Mexía arrived safely at Veracruz before June 1. Within a day or two they learned that a friend was to be executed in Mexico City for political reasons, and fearing for their lives, they offered the captain of the small merchant schooner *United States* $500 to sail immediately to New Orleans. After a voyage of six days on board the uncomfortable craft, they entered the mouth of the Mississippi River on June 7, 1830.

They transferred to a steamboat towing vessels upstream and reached New Orleans three days later. Zavala found a number of former acquaintances in the Crescent City, and some wrote letters of introduction to influential persons in the Northeast. He added these letters to those he had collected in Mexico City from Poinsett and his successor, Anthony Butler.

Zavala and Mexía boarded the luxurious steamboat *Louisiana* on June 16 for the trip up the Mississippi River to Louisville, Kentucky. Staterooms on the upper decks were comfortable with beds, washstands, and mirrors; Zavala thought $40 for the 1200-mile trip was money well spent.

In his journal, Zavala made observations about people he met, places he visited, and historical and environmental information gathered from popular travel books such as those of Timothy Flint and Mrs. Frances Trollope. Like those writers, Zavala expected to publish the account of his travels and observations about life in the United States for circulation in Mexico. At Louisville, Zavala and Mexía changed to a smaller boat for the thirty miles to Cincinnati, arriving there on June 27.

President Andrew Jackson visited Cincinnati the next day, and using the letter of introduction from Anthony Butler, a Jackson appointee, Zavala and Mexía called on the patriarch. Jackson expressed regret over the collapse of the Guerrero government and predicted that the people would eventually triumph.

The pair continued up the river and celebrated the Fourth of July on board the steamer. During the ceremony Zavala offered this toast:

> Mexican citizens express their good wishes for liberty wherever they may be. . . . Hear then my wishes: That providence maintain this people in its present institutions for many centuries, and that Mexico may imitate it successfully.

At Wheeling (West Virginia, then Virginia) the friends separated, Mexía for Washington while Zavala continued en route to New York. Zavala chose the opportunity to make a grand tour, probably on advice from Poinsett, who had visited the same area. He traveled by stagecoach north to Lake Erie, paused to visit Niagara Falls, then continued by boat to Montreal and Quebec. The Yucatecan returned to Montreal where he took the stage south to connect with a steamer on Lake Champlain and then transferred to another on Lake George. From there he rode a coach to Saratoga where he was presented to the exiled Joseph Bonaparte, the former King of Spain, who was vacationing at the springs from his home near Trenton, New Jersey. Continuing southward, Zavala reached Albany where a steamer took him down the Hudson River. Quite by chance Zavala met the Mexía family at West Point on July 25; they had come up from New York

City to see the military school. The steamer reached the city before dark and Zavala took a room at Mrs. Street's boarding house on Broadway.

Zavala had an immediate reunion with seventeen-year-old Lorenzo, Jr. "Nothing can compare," the father wrote, "to the pleasant . . . impression that one gets . . . when a man sees the heir of his name . . . [and] image" after a long absence. Since 1827 the youth had been at the large and popular boys' boarding school operated by the Perrignet brothers north of the city. Zavala had made the arrangements while he was governor, and Lorenzo, Jr., and two friends, Bernardo and Genaro Peón, had traveled together from Yucatán to Havana and New York. In August, Zavala, his son, and Genaro Peón went to Philadelphia to meet Poinsett; they remained two weeks discussing Zavala's land business and seeing the sights. Zavala then visited Mexía in Baltimore and continued to Washington where he was able to meet many prominent men. He even dined with President Jackson and Secretary of State Martin Van Buren.

Poinsett accompanied Zavala and his son to Boston at the end of August to meet William H. Sumner, lawyer, former legislator, and currently adjutant general of Massachusetts. He was one of the investors in a New York syndicate, known as the Galveston Bay and Texas Land Company, interested in acquiring Texas land. On the way they paused at Northampton, Massachusetts, to enroll Lorenzo, Jr., in Round Hill School, an outstanding institution established in 1823 by noted educator Joseph Green Cogswell and historian George Bancroft. Zavala was back in New York by September 16; he attended a banquet observing the twentieth anniversary of the Grito de Dolores that signaled the beginning of the movement for Mexican independence. Among the political refugees at the celebration were Generals Pedro Celestino Negrete, José Antonio de Echavarri, and Mexía.

For the next month, Zavala concentrated on completing the sale of his empresario contract to the Galveston Bay and

Texas Land Company. Company officers were less interested in colonization than the potential profits from the acquisition of land in southeastern Texas should the United States acquire Texas as they anticipated. The directors had also secured the rights to two other grants contiguous with Zavala's: those of Ohio resident, David G. Burnet, and Mexico City merchant, Joseph Vehlein.

This joint stock company, led by Anthony Dey of New York City, an attorney and counselor, modeled its venture on systems established by earlier land speculators in Kentucky, Tennessee, and Mississippi. John P. Austin, a New York merchant, wrote his cousin, Stephen F. Austin, in December 1830:

> From what I can learn it is the most extensive land Company that was ever known in this or any other Country . . . and its board of Directors is composed of the most respectable and influential men among us.

The company's supposed acquisition — 16,000 square miles, more than ten million acres — included twenty present-day southeastern Texas counties west of the Sabine River from just north of the old Nacogdoches-San Antonio road (present Highway 21) to the Gulf of Mexico. The western boundary was Stephen F. Austin's colony along the Brazos River watershed. The area included the old Spanish town of Nacogdoches and scattered settlements of Anglo American squatters. The latter had been promised titles by the state of Coahuila-Texas in 1828 but they still lacked deeds because of the political turmoil in Mexico City. The Galveston Bay Company expected to incorporate the resident Anglo squatters into their allotted 1200 settlers.

Vehlein and Burnet had acquired their empresario contracts from the state of Coahuila-Texas in December 1826. Each was allowed the standard six years in which to settle 300 families along the lower Trinity valley and around

Nacogdoches, respectively. Vehlein received a second contract in 1828 permitting him to colonize 100 more families along the eastern shore of Galveston Bay. Vehlein never visited Texas, sent no families, and almost immediately named John Lucius Woodbury his agent to dispose of the contract. Woodbury, a New Yorker, may have been Vehlein's business partner in 1826. Woodbury started for the United States in 1829 but died by May 1830, leaving his son, Jesse, to carry out the business.

Burnet, a native of New Jersey, was living in Cincinnati where one brother was mayor and another a member of the Ohio Supreme Court. The family was politically conservative and deplored both Jeffersonian and Jacksonian democracy, a philosophy that affected Burnet's activities in Texas. Unhappy as a merchant and lawyer, Burnet visited Stephen F. Austin in Texas in 1826, and after securing letters of introduction, journeyed to Saltillo to apply for an empresario grant. Expecting to profit as an empresario, Burnet returned to Ohio to seek colonists and financial backers. However, the political turmoil after the Mexican election and the 1829 Spanish invasion doomed his efforts. Burnet's jurist brother, Jacob, became a United States senator in 1828, and David urged him to persuade his colleagues to buy eastern Texas (which would include his grant) from Mexico. Acquiring this part of Texas was a popular idea among many men in the United States, including President Andrew Jackson. By March 1830, however, Burnet was negotiating the sale of his contract in New York and probably had met Woodbury and Joel R. Poinsett, who was beginning his search for capital for the Zavala project.

Even as the Galveston Bay and Texas Land Company was planning to acquire the empresario contracts of Burnet, Vehlein, and Zavala, the Mexican government ordered an end to emigration from the United States. Mexicans had inherited Spanish xenophobia and remembered when the United States seized Baton Rouge and Mobile from Spain between 1810 and 1813. Also President Jackson, then a general, had invaded Spanish Pensacola to punish renegades in 1818. Thus a quixotic rebellion by Anglo Americans in Nacogdoches at the close of 1826 aroused suspicion that the United States again intended to send adventurers to infiltrate and rebel, which would lead to the annexation of eastern Texas. The Fredonia Rebellion at Nacogdoches was quickly suppressed by Mexican troops from San Antonio augmented by Anglo militia from Austin's colony. As a result, a permanent garrison was established at Nacogdoches to monitor the old Spanish road entering Texas from Natchitoches, Louisiana, and to observe local troublemakers.

Subsequently, a fact-finding expedition into Texas in 1828 revealed that everywhere east of San Antonio Anglo Americans outnumbered native Mexicans. Moreover, most spoke only English and were not being assimilated into Mexican culture as had been expected in the colonization plans. The authorities perceived the situation to be an immediate threat to national security. In Mexico City, Anthony Butler, who replaced Poinsett as U. S. minister, was offering to buy eastern Texas—perhaps as far west as the Brazos River—which was considered an insult to Mexico. If Mexico refused to sell, would the long-expected invasion across the Sabine River take place? The centralist administration urged Congress to act, and on April 6, 1830, a law banned further immigration into Texas except by Europeans or native Mexicans.

Stephen F. Austin won a reprieve for his colony and that of Green DeWitt at Gonzales, using a technicality in the wording of the law that suggested that "established" colonies were exempt. With the help of Mexican friends, Austin successfully argued that his and DeWitt's colonies were established because both had settled at least 100 families, which by the colonization law permitted a state-appointed land commissioner to issue titles. By this reasoning, all incomplete contracts where no titles had been issued—such as those of Burnet,

Vehlein, and Zavala—could be settled in the future only by European and Mexican families.

The Mexican authorities placed an even greater restriction on Zavala's contract. Even when first issued by Coahuila-Texas in 1829, it had to be approved by the national executive because the grant lay within the fifty-two-mile-wide boundary reserve and the twenty-six-mile-wide coastal reserve forbidden to foreigners. With the centralists now in power, their suspicions about Zavala's intentions caused Congress to add a proviso in May 1830 to his existing contract requiring lists of all potential settlers to screen any natives of the United States.

Zavala, once so interested in formulating a national colonization law, never considered being an active empresario like Austin. Nor was he interested in settling native Mexicans in Texas. From the first application, he viewed an empresario contract in Texas as a salable property as demonstrated by naming Luckett his agent in June 1828 to find investors in the United States. But like David G. Burnet, Luckett found few investors willing to risk capital in a country beset with political coups and European invaders.

Impatient with Luckett's slow progress, Zavala signed a contract with Poinsett in December 1829 revoking the Luckett arrangement. As Zavala's agent, Poinsett was to "sell, mortgage, trade, lease, convey, or bestow" titles to Zavala's land in Texas.

This scheme violated state and national colonization laws and was therefore illegal. Zavala seemed unaware, or unconcerned, that only a state-appointed land commissioner could issue titles or that an empresario owned none of the land within his grant and was unable to charge settlers for their land. Empresarios only advertised for colonists and screened applicants.

Coahuila-Texas allowed each head of a family one league (4,428 acres) if a rancher, and one labor (177 acres) of irrigable land if a farmer. Anglo Texans usually claimed to be both and thus received 4,605 acres. Colonists paid standard fees totaling just under $200 to the state, the land commissioner, the surveyor, and the clerk for writing the deed on special stamped paper. The only remuneration for an empresario was 23,027 acres of land awarded him by the state for each 100 families he settled.

Thus Zavala's reward would have been 115,135 acres if he located 500 families within the six years allowed in his contract. He could locate this "premium" land anywhere within his colony and sell it to latecomers for whatever they would pay. The buyers of the premium land, however, had to become Mexican citizens and live on and improve the land. Coahuila-Texas wanted no absentee landlords. This lengthy process was too slow, however, for Zavala, who lacked capital for long-term gains. Zavala's need for money overcame his earlier idealism about colonization and resident land ownership. He doubtless convinced himself that he was doing nothing that others had not already done.

Besides involving Poinsett in the scheme, Zavala also gave the new United States minister, Anthony Butler, an interest in his contract. On March 10, 1830, Butler and Zavala signed a contract to create a company to settle 500 families on Zavala's Sabine River land. Butler would be a director, and the profits would be divided between Zavala, Poinsett, and Butler.

Butler was playing a double game, trying to acquire personal property in an area that he hoped to annex to the United States. His superior, Secretary of State Martin Van Buren, warned the new minister in October 1829 that Zavala had been given a valuable tract that "was within the bounds of the district whose cession to the United States is to form the subject of negotiation between the two countries." President Jackson, he added, hoped that Mexico would "extinguish" Zavala's contract before cession of the territory was made to the United States so as not to be part of any reparations. It was a good thing for Zavala's peace of mind when he met President Jackson in Cincinnati in July 1830 that Butler had not revealed Jackson's concern.

When Poinsett reached the United States in early 1830, he discovered that Luckett had just completed preliminary arrangements to sell Zavala's land. Worried about the legality of the new partnership, Poinsett notified Butler in March that he had received a letter from New York lawyer Anthony Dey, concerning the Zavala contract. Meanwhile, passage of the restrictive April 6, 1830, law banning Anglo American immigration meant that whoever owned the contract would have to find European settlers. Tornel, the Mexican minister in Washington, published the law in United States newspapers and warned Anglo Americans not to go to Texas.

Upon arriving in New York in July, Zavala at first disavowed Luckett's negotiations with the Galveston Bay speculators, but after meeting Dey and Sumner he changed his mind. To appease Poinsett and Butler, Zavala arranged for the company to give them an unstated number of certificates for leagues and labors of land (4,428 and 177 acres). These same kind of certificates were given to investors in the company. The three empresarios—Zavala, Burnet, and Vehlein—each received a cash settlement and similar land certificates. The participants revealed no details about the amounts they secured, but President Jackson heard that Zavala received $100,000.

In December the Galveston Bay Company and Zavala sent carefully worded letters explaining the transactions to the secretary of state in Mexico City, the governor of Coahuila-Texas, and Stephen F. Austin. The company assured everyone that the three empresarios were still closely involved in the enterprise with large holdings and were cooperating in all plans. This, of course, was not the case. At the same time, the directors issued a veiled warning that the trio had executed irrevocable indentures making Anthony Dey, William H. Sumner, and George Curtis trustees to handle the affairs of the three colonies.

Zavala's letter to Governor Viesca of Coahuila-Texas, a federalist friend, explained that he had formed the company to send European colonists to Texas. Some, he said, would leave

New York within the month. By the attached documents, Viesca would "be informed of my actions, which will help to dissipate any sinister interpretations which my eternal enemies . . . have attempted to give to my steps in this event." Rumors had spread in Mexico that when Zavala left Mexico City after his dismissal from office, he had threatened to spark revolution in Texas. Nothing in extant correspondence confirms such a charge. Zavala addressed a similar letter in Spanish to Austin, adding that he would soon leave for France to seek European colonists.

Mexía was also involved with the Galveston Bay Company. In December the trustees employed him as agent and lobbyist to go to Saltillo and Mexico City to urge that the ban against emigration from the United States be annulled. The company's directors revealed their lack of understanding of the colonization laws when they told Mexía to persuade Austin to charge the same price for land as did the Galveston Bay Company—five to ten cents an acre. Austin, of course, did not charge for the land. When Mexía retired, the trustees hoped he would settle in Texas as their land commissioner, another impossibility unless the state of Coahuila-Texas named him to that post.

Mexía also held an interest in the Union Company, a subcontractor of the Galveston Bay associates. He recruited Monsieur Adolphe Decaen, a grape grower, and several French, Swiss, and German families already in the United States to sail to Galveston Bay in early 1831. Mexía's contracts with immigrants reveal one way the speculators intended to profit from colonists: each settler signed a three-year contract to work five days a week for the company in exchange for transporting his family to Texas, a 177-acre farm site at no cost, and a wage of $60 per year. The Europeans, overjoyed to own a sizeable farm, did not realize that Coahuila-Texas awarded headrights of 4,605 acres to all immigrant families. The naive settler willingly signed a release giving the company the balance of that headright—4,428 acres.

When ships with Mexía's colonists and those of the Galveston Bay Company (including a number of Anglo American workmen) arrived in Texas in early 1831, the local military commander at Anahuac refused to allow company agents to settle families, claiming their presence violated the 1830 law. Most of the unfortunate recruits returned to the United States, though a few Germans remained, hoping that the problem would be solved. This unexpected development forced the speculators to cancel their plans until the centralist administration changed in Mexico City and/or the April 1830 law could be annulled.

Meanwhile, Zavala was unconcerned about colonists. He had fallen in love during the autumn. Estranged from his wife for a number of years, Zavala doubtless had entered into amorous affairs during his time in Mexico City. Apparently he was an admirer of beautiful women. In his *Viage a los Estados-Unidos*, published in 1834, he said that Mexican travelers were always surprised by the beauty of Anglo American women. With their "good color, large bright eyes, well-shaped hands and feet . . . " they were unusually attractive although they lacked the voluptuous walk of Mexican women. Now at age forty-two, he met a beautiful, tall, dark-eyed New York native half his age.

During his early morning walks in Battery Park near his boardinghouse, Zavala regularly noticed the attractive young woman with two small children. After discreet inquiry, he learned that her name was Mrs. Miranda West Cresswell. After a proper introduction, the young widow enjoyed the attention from the cosmopolitan gentleman. Like Pygmalion and Galatea, Zavala began educating her to suit his more sophisticated taste by giving "her an accomplished education," according to gossips. He even changed her first name to Emily, according to a note in his journal.

On December 22, the pair sailed for France where Zavala was to recruit colonists for the Galveston Bay Company. Upon reaching Paris in February, Zavala bought "Madame

Zavala" new clothes, subscribed to English and French newspapers, and contracted to print 5,000 copies of his *Ensayo Histórico de las Revoluciones de Megico desde 1808 hasta 1830*. He had worked on this first volume of his history for the past several years.

Zavala enjoyed himself in Paris and managed to contact many influential French leaders who quizzed him about Mexican politics and land speculation. But he secured no colonists. Always looking for income, he became an agent for a group of Spanish emigrées living in Paris but with business in London. A lawsuit indicated that they were disappointed in his representation between March and May, but Zavala moved on to other things. His activities are not well documented and he may have traveled to other countries.

When Zavala's enemies in Mexico City learned about his companion, one publicly labeled him a vagabond and a libertine. From Mexico City, Mexía warned his friend that rumors about him were spreading around the capital. Zavala's wife had died in Yucatán in April 1831, and he should have received the news in Paris in May or June. Whether her death triggered the gossip is unknown. The trustees had expected him to return to New York by July, and they complained to Mexía that Zavala was using the funds advanced for recruiting colonists for other purposes. Perhaps they asked him to return.

Zavala sailed from Le Havre on the *François I* and reached New York on November 10. He rented rooms for one month at Mrs. Ann Stagg's Washington Avenue boardinghouse on the suburban west side of Manhattan Island. Anthony Dey, James Prentiss (of the Union Company), and others immediately visited Zavala to discuss the colonial project. At their request, Zavala wrote to Acting President Bustamante (his former political enemy) on November 15, complaining that the commandant general for Texas had acted improperly the previous spring when he refused to allow "Zavala's" colonists to settle on his empresario grant. This was Zavala's last act as an empresario. Meanwhile, everyone hoped for a change in administrations.

Personal business required Zavala's attention on Saturday, November 12, his second day in New York. Early in the morning he visited Father Félix Varela, the pastor of the Catholic church on Ann Street, about performing a marriage ceremony for himself and Emily, who was seven months pregnant. The couple returned to the church at eight that evening and the priest gave them his "nuptial benedictions." Zavala dutifully noted these details in his journal.

The next month the Zavalas moved to the home of John Collet, a French druggist, on Greenwich Street not far from Mrs. Stagg's rooming house. Emily delivered a son there on January 1, 1832, and Zavala named him Agustín for his own older brother. Lorenzo, Jr., now eighteen years old and only four years younger than his stepmother, had finished school and joined the family as his father's secretary. The family was further increased when Zavala adopted Emily's son Henry, now age four. On May 11, the Zavalas went to Father Varela for the baptism of Agustín and Henry accompanied by federalist friends, José Salgado and his wife, who served as godparents. In June the family moved to Brooklyn.

Zavala had used this time to polish volume two of his *Ensayo Histórico*; it appeared in print in early 1832. By this time the political situation in Mexico had improved for the federalists. General Santa Anna had begun a revolution in Veracruz against President Bustamente's centralist regime on January 2, 1832. Zavala wrote, "The fire has been lit, and God knows where it will stop." Mexía, who had joined Santa Anna, urged Zavala to hurry back and stand for election to the Congress. Zavala yearned to return despite standing orders for his arrest should he set foot on Mexican soil.

Zavala visited Philadelphia in April where he heard his old enemy, former president-elect, Gómez Pedraza, denounce Acting President Bustamante. The legitimately elected president of 1828 had been a refugee in the United States ever

since Zavala's revolt in December 1829. The two men managed to overcome their political differences, and two months
later, the pragmatic Zavala urged the deposed president to
reclaim his office. Zavala told Gómez Pedraza that he was the
only man who could unite the country and end the raging
civil war between the federalist and centralist factions. The
two implacable enemies of 1828 began plotting their return to
power by burying the past. Once more Zavala might be able
to engineer a compromise and a coalition for the good of the
nation—and himself.

Zavala wrote a somewhat poignant letter to Poinsett from
Philadelphia. As a historian and philosopher, he admired the
stability of the United States. Citizens and politicians there
argued their differences over the tariff, the national bank, and
diplomatic affairs without resorting to war. How different in
Mexico! There "we are condemned to a series of bloody revolutions." Then he added, "I may be one of the victims . . . ."

Zavala left Emily and the children with Lorenzo, Jr., in
Brooklyn and by August was in Veracruz with fellow refugees,
José Salgado and Father José María Alpuche. He penned a
letter to Santa Anna on August 12 after the general complained that he had not heard from him. As an apology for
what he had said and written about Santa Anna since 1829,
Zavala rationalized that nobody has "either pure vices or pure
virtues." The person with the fewest vices and who committed the fewest errors was the best. He added that the road facing them "should be traveled with reserve and circumspec-
tion, although always with good faith."

Zavala, Gómez Pedraza, and Santa Anna reached a pragmatic agreement: Gómez Pedraza would assume the presidency while Zavala would reoccupy the governorship of the
State of Mexico. Santa Anna, ready to march against Puebla,
ordered General Gabriel Valencia and Colonels Mexía and
Juan Arago to occupy Toluca, now the capital of the state of
Mexico. On October 23, they forced the acting governor to
flee, while Bustamante's supporters retreated into Mexico

City for a last stand. Zavala occupied the governor's office on November 1 and called the legislature, dissolved earlier by the national Congress, into session. His liberal reform administration was so well remembered that most cities and villages welcomed him back.

Zavala remained in control of Toluca for only thirty-five days before centralist troops approached on December 5 and he again fled to the hills. Within two weeks, he recruited 1000 men and recaptured Toluca. This brief military exercise earned him the title of "General." On December 23, 1832, the centralists capitulated at the village of Zavaleta near Puebla. The agreement reached between the contenders extended amnesty to all offenders since February 1, 1828, allowed Gómez Pedraza to complete the presidential term to which he had been elected in 1828, and provided for regular elections to be held so that a new president would be installed in April. Zavala was represented at the peace table by his old friends, Andrés Quintana Roo and José María Héredia.

Zavala and Mexía sent for their families, who traveled together from New York to Veracruz. Lorenzo, Jr., continued to Toluca to serve his father as an aide while Emily and Charlotte Mexía remained on the coast with the younger children. Early in 1833 the women and children, escorted by ten soldiers, went by litter to Orizaba. There they spent a few days with Señora Gómez Pedraza who was waiting to join her husband in Mexico City. After a few days' rest, the Zavala and Mexía families traveled by coach to Mexico City where Charlotte Mexía's sister lived. Emily and her sons continued on to Toluca the next day to join the governor.

After two years in exile Zavala looked forward to the future of his state and nation. The economic problems, however, would be difficult to solve in his bankrupt homeland. Moreover, he knew that the political ambitions of the defeated centralist party would emerge again in the same violent manner. The philosopher could only wonder when it would happen.

CHAPTER 5

Zavala and
Santa Anna's
Presidency, 1833-1835

GOVERNOR ZAVALA rode into Mexico City on January 3, 1833, to watch General Santa Anna and President Gómez Pedraza make their triumphal entry into the capital. The shrewd general soon retired to his hacienda between Veracruz and Jalapa to await his inevitable election to the presidency. The state legislatures met on February 15 and voted for senators and the executive branch. When Congress convened at the end of March to count the ballots, the federalist slate of Santa Anna and Valentín Gómez Farías won by a wide margin.

A master at holding the public's attention, Santa Anna claimed he was ill and unable to attend his inauguration in Mexico City on April 1. Thus Vice President Gómez Farías, a sincere liberal idealist from Zacatecas and much admired for his integrity, served as acting president until fall and began many federalist reforms. Historians continue to debate Santa

Anna's commitment to reform at this time: did he callously allow his federalist vice president to propose reforms targeting the long-envied *fueros* (privileges) of the Church and the military which provided special tribunals and freedom from taxation? Did Santa Anna expect that such changes would destroy Gómez Farías' political career? Santa Anna resumed and relinquished the presidency several times between April 1833 and March 1834, and the vice president presumed his actions were approved by the chief executive.

Meanwhile Governor Zavala was at work restoring federalist reforms in his state surrounding volatile Mexico City. Resuming office one month after his forty-fourth birthday, he understood only too well that life was short and unpredictable. Therefore he worked hard to create within a matter of months a new system that reflected his liberal idealism. He focused on improving the lives of the poor by education, better roads and canals, and redistribution of the land. At this time he believed that educating the underclass would turn them into responsible citizens who would appreciate the value of a republic like that of the United States. Zavala's tactics angered the established elite, but dispassionate historians view this creative period as a tribute to his genius. They see his initiatives as the foundation for La Reforma, the changes made by Benito Juarez in the 1850s.

Zavala served as de facto governor from November 1832 to February 1833, when the legislature elected him to a four-year term commencing March 12. One of Zavala's first actions was to resume the land reforms that he had begun in 1827. On December 31, 1832, he seized the vast estate of the Duke of Monteleone y Terranova, a descendant of conquistador Hernán Cortes, who resided in Spain. Zavala's predecessor had not followed the 1828 national law to confiscate such property, an oversight that permitted the centralist regime to use the Duke's income to preserve the status quo of the aristocratic party. Zavala intended to make the land public domain, and any funds secured by expropriation would be used to build roads and extend public education. The legislature nationalized the Duke's property in April and divided the funds between the state treasury and the *ayuntamientos* in which the properties lay.

A keen politician and a student of history, Zavala was applying Napoleon's land confiscation programs to Mexico. One Mexican economic historian, Andrés Molina Enríquez, postulated in 1933 that Zavala understood that Napoleon's success came in part from this redistribution of the nobility's property to the peasants. Zavala's plan, he said, might have solved Mexico's greatest problem in the 1830s had it been used nationwide against absentee landlords.

The major agrarian reform during Zavala's administration was nationalizing the Philippine missions owned by the Dominican order. The legislature passed the law on March 29, 1833, dividing arable mission land into equal plots, each large enough to support a family. The government leased tracts annually to farmers for five percent of the appraised value; the rental income financed irrigation canals, roads, and public education. Only poor residents of the state could apply for farms, with preference given to Indians and veterans of the wars for independence. State employees and their families could not acquire this land, and uncultivated tracts reverted to the state for redistribution after three years.

Zavala was disappointed but not surprised that his public Literary Institute and the state library had been neglected by his predecessor. The school, unequaled in Mexico, had disintegrated, and its pupils dispersed to religious academies. The library had been stripped—no new books had been purchased and few of the originals remained. The conservative priest serving as library director under the centralist regime destroyed 380 volumes including works by Gibbon, Hume, Bacon, Madame de Stael, Montesquieu, Bentham, Adam Smith, Diderot, Voltaire, Volney, Rousseau, Helvetius, and others. Zavala asked the legislature to replace basic works and scientific volumes.

Governor Zavala was pleasantly surprised by the cooperation of state legislators in 1833. Members also approved his
plans to reorganize the treasury, regulate the local militia and
the courts, and seize more ecclesiastic property. During these
weeks, Zavala also excluded the clergy from primary education, abolished the tobacco monopoly, and established an
official newspaper, *Reformador*. In April, the legislature
named him citizen *"benemérito* of the state in heroic degree."

In May 1833, however, the centralists staged a revolt in
neighboring Michoacán, demanding that the rights and privileges of the army and the Church be restored. When Zavala
heard about the requests to resume the special privileges in
the courts and from taxation, he could not believe that "those
two forces needed any defense." He told the residents that it
was their decision whether they wished to be free or servile,
and he asked citizens and officials to stand by his reforms.
Their choice, he explained dramatically, was between fire
and water, slavery and liberty, ignominy and glory, supersti-
tion and philosophy, ignorance and enlightenment. This
didactic summons reflected Zavala's immersion in the writings of his favorite authors.

There was sufficient centralist support, however, that
General Gabriel Durán raised a revolt on June 1 in Tlalpam,
Zavala's former home. Besides demanding the return of
"religión y fueros," he wanted to void Zavala's executive
actions since November and return former Governor
Melchor Múzquiz to office. Durán also urged Santa Anna to
take charge of the presidency. Santa Anna instead assumed
command of a federalist army gathered in Mexico City. The
enigmatic president, however, named a known centralist,
General Mariano Arista, as his second in command.

Zavala protested the appointment of Arista, and his suspicions proved correct when Arista joined Durán. The two conservative officers supposedly offered Santa Anna the dictator-
ship of the nation, and when he declined, they "detained"
him. Believing that Santa Anna was a prisoner, Zavala and

Gómez Farías quickly rallied a federalist force to rescue him. The quasi-arrest of Santa Anna was perhaps a ploy of his own doing to test public opinion.

In any event, Santa Anna escaped his captors and fled to Mexico City. Once in the capital, the wily president became convinced it was not time for a centralist uprising, not even to rescue religion. Santa Anna therefore pursued Durán into Guanajuato where the unlucky "rebels" surrendered. Ultimately, a number of generals and the centralist figure-head, former Vice President (and Acting President) Busta-mante, were banished from Mexico.

Zavala acted quickly after Durán's pronouncement in June. He called the legislature into special session to deal with the crisis. The members gave him almost dictatorial powers to float a loan, seize the property of those supporting the centralist rebels, dismiss employees and banish suspicious persons, and call up the civil militia.

At this same time, a major epidemic of cholera erupted throughout Mexico. Aware of Zavala's medical knowledge, the state legislature authorized him to take whatever steps were necessary to control the disease. The lawmakers created a board of health and gave Zavala regulatory powers over it, along with unlimited funds. His work as a physician during the crisis earned praise for his devotion. When cholera struck Toluca, Zavala sent his wife and small children to Charlotte Mexía in Mexico City. Emily had yet to master Spanish, and she enjoyed being with Charlotte who was fluent in both lan-guages. Cholera also pervaded the capital, but Emily remained at the Mexía residence until fall.

Governor Zavala also took part in national politics. Mexía had asked a Yucatecan friend in January to have Yucatán name Zavala a representative to the national Congress. Times had changed on the peninsula and Zavala's candidacy was endorsed; Congress accepted Zavala's credentials in the lower house on March 23, 1833. However, the legislature of the State of Mexico prevented him from attending. Its members denied him permission to leave and told Congress that his leadership was needed at Toluca during the spring and summer.

Zavala's friends in Congress, equally anxious for his talents, asked the executive branch to demand his presence. "You, dear friend," wrote Mexía, recently elected senator from the State of Mexico, "are the only regenerating genius and you ought to make every effort to come and organize this decadent structure." The conservatives complained that the new federalist-dominated Congress was inexperienced and its members came only to promote change. One aristocrat sneered, "The majority of the members . . . put on a dress coat, or a Prince Albert and gloves, for the first time . . . when they attended the opening . . . session."

The state prevailed, however, and Zavala remained in Toluca until fall. Nevertheless Zavala outlined an extremely liberal national program that he hoped Acting President Gómez Farías would incorporate into his plans. Zavala envisioned a national convention to discuss major changes: preservation of the federal system, popular elections, absolute freedom of the press and religion, abolition of the *fueros*, reorganization of the army, free trade throughout the nation, a reduction in exorbitant government salaries, removal of the national capital to a smaller town away from the influence of wealthy lobbyists, and a statement defining the rights of the people. Obviously, his exile in the United States had sharpened his desire to protect and increase the rights of individuals.

Confident that his state reform program was underway, Zavala asked for and received permission to leave the state in September, although his resignation was not accepted. By October 3, his birthday, he had taken his seat in the chamber of deputies. His wife and children, of course, were already in the capital with the Mexía family.

Zavala arrived just in time to vote for reforms requested by the people of Texas. Stephen F. Austin had reached the capital in July with Texas petitions asking for separate statehood from union with Coahuila, a repeal of the ban on Anglo American immigration, and an extension of the exemption from the national tariff. Congress was recessed, and the cholera epidemic had driven many leaders out of the capital. Unwell and upset by rumors that cholera was devastating Texas, Austin became impatient when Congress met in September but failed to act quickly on the Texas issues. He told Gómez Farías that the Texans would not submit to further delay; the acting president became angry, assuming that Austin meant that the Texans would declare their independence. On October 2 in a dark mood, Austin wrote a letter to San Antonio urging the *ayuntamientos* to organize a separate state in case Congress denied their petition. This sedition would cause Austin's arrest in January 1834 and his long confinement in Mexico City until July 1835.

When Zavala arrived, he met with Austin to discuss Texas affairs. By the end of October, Congress voted to repeal the ban on Anglo American immigration. Implementation, however, was delayed until May 21, 1834.

Unrestricted immigration into Texas stimulated Zavala to try new ventures in Texas land since he no longer had any financial interest in the Galveston Bay Company. Senator Victor Blanco of Coahuila-Texas, attending the current session, offered to sell a portion of his eleven-league grant in Texas, acquired in 1830 when the state offered these 48,708-acre tracts at low rates (less than two cents per acre) to native Mexicans to encourage Hispanic immigration. Blanco had asked Austin to locate suitable tracts in his colony, one of which was five leagues (22,140 acres) on the upper San Jacinto River near present-day Lake Houston in Harris County. Blanco was probably the agent for his Saltillo friend, Fernando del Valle, who also had a similar eleven-league (48,708 acres) grant for sale along the lower Trinity River in present Leon and Houston counties. Both men had received titles from a fellow federalist, José Fransisco Madero, in 1831 during his brief tenure as state land commissioner from eastern Texas. Zavala perhaps acquired the combined sixteen leagues (70,848 acres), undeveloped, for as little as five cents an acre, the lowest price being asked by the Galveston Bay Company. If so, the total price was about $3,500. The Trinity River land was sold in 1837 for about $12,000.

All of the Texas requests except separate statehood were granted by Congress during the fall session. Zavala had told Austin that he supported the statehood petition, but on November 3, he abruptly, and without explanation, changed his mind in favor of making Texas a territory. Feeling betrayed, Austin told Zavala that he would protest making Texas a territory subject to rule by the national government. Zavala remained silent. He did not tell the empresario that Santa Anna wanted Texas to be a territory. Nobody dared to oppose the president. "This has made me *a goodly number of enemies* here who wished for a Territory," Austin wrote to his associate in Texas, *"nada importa* — all will go right." Events proved him wrong — within a month he was under arrest because of his October letter urging unilateral action for statehood.

Zavala was more concerned with implementing national reforms. His longtime hatred of the ecclesiastical hierarchy led him to attack the power and privileges of the Church. He believed that the national financial problems could be solved only by the confiscation of Church lands. By controlling Church property, the government could solve its own financial problems and support the Church. He introduced a bill on November 7 creating an office of public credit to oversee the sequestration of ecclesiastical property and advocating suppression of the regular clergy. Churchmen tried to bribe Zavala, but he rejected the offers. While his suggestions did not become law immediately, Acting President Gómez Farías incorporated some of Zavala's ideas into reform measures after the Yucatecan had left for France.

Zavala's appointment as minister to the French court was

both a well-deserved honor and a way to isolate the liberal reformer, a fact that Zavala was slow to realize. Under the restored Bourbon kings, France had refused to recognize the Mexican Republic during the 1820s. When Louis Philippe, the Duke of Orleans, was installed as the "Citizen King" by the Chamber of Deputies in July 1830, the situation changed. The first French minister arrived in Mexico in January 1833, and Gómez Farías immediately named Zavala representative to the Paris court. Political maneuvering delayed placing his name before the Senate until the end of May, and it was October 17 before his appointment was approved.

The secretary of state prepared instructions for Zavala on October 28, but for unknown reasons he did not receive them until November 26, 1833. It is clear that he was packed and ready to depart because four days later the Zavala family left Mexico City. Zavala regretted leaving his state and national reforms in the hands of others, but the appointment to the French court offered a new challenge. Not only was it an honor and a reward for faithful service, but also the post was a new opportunity to serve his country. Had he suspected that he would never return to Mexico City, the departure would have been devastating.

The family and members of the legation staff reached Veracruz on December 5 and sailed for New York thirteen days later. After an uneventful voyage they reached Manhattan on January 6, 1834. Emily, still in her early twenties, gave birth to her third child and first daughter, María Emilia, on February 2, and Father Varela baptized the infant two weeks later. Anxious about both his wife and the legation, Zavala had sent the staff to Paris on February 1 to prepare the way while the family followed at the end of the month. After a fast crossing of less than the usual four weeks, the family reached their quarters at #67 Rue de la Universite, Faubourg St. Germaine, on March 28.

The Mexican minister's arrival at Le Havre had not been smooth. Although Tomás Murphy, the Mexican charge d'affaires in Paris, had requested the necessary visas in February, Zavala was not accorded the usual diplomatic immunities at the customs house. Upon arriving in Paris the coolness continued when his official reception by King Louis Philippe was delayed until April 26. By way of contrast, his Spanish counterpart had been received only three days after his arrival. After the formality, however, Zavala moved confidently through the diplomatic community.

Zavala and Emily enjoyed themselves in Paris, attending diplomatic functions, the opera, the theater, visiting historic places, and traveling to Belgium and the lower Rhine Valley. While in Paris, Emily sat for a portrait in her court gown and the formal, high-hair arrangement dictated by fashion. A vain woman, throughout her life Emily treasured wardrobe items acquired in Paris. Her descendants gave the San Jacinto Museum of History at the battleground a black silk chiffon evening shawl and a stylish straw hat that she had worn as the wife of the Mexican minister to France. Likewise, Zavala's formal uniform trimmed in gold lace and his dress sword worn in Paris became family heirlooms.

Spain still had not recognized Mexico's independence in 1834, and though Zavala had not been entrusted to negotiate official recognition, he devoted much effort toward that goal while he was in Paris. Before he left New York he heard rumors that Mexico would declare war on Spain if independence was not acknowledged. Such careless statements upset him, not only for diplomatic reasons, but also because he knew that Mexico could ill afford such an undertaking.

French newspapers reported that Zavala had come to Paris to negotiate recognition of Mexican independence, rumors planted perhaps by Spanish diplomats who indeed favored such a step. Concluding that Spain wanted to gain a reputation for liberalism in order to work more closely with France and Great Britain, Zavala realized that Spain was more eager to recognize Mexican independence (and the other Spanish-American republics) than vice versa. He immediately urged

*Emily de Zavala, a portrait probably made in Paris in 1834
(courtesy Center for American History, University of Texas
at Austin).*

President Santa Anna to give such a commission to one of Mexico's European diplomats, but he tactfully did not ask to be appointed.

Zavala met informally with representatives from the Spanish-American republics to discuss Spain's new interest in recognizing their independence. They agreed that it was up to Spain to initiate the move, but gradually Zavala's attitude softened. When it became evident that Spain must concede recognition, Zavala urged his Western Hemisphere colleagues to take the first steps. This would save Spanish pride from unnecessary mortification, he said, and gain them more in the long run.

By June, after more letters to Mexico City urging the appointment of a special commissioner to negotiate with the Spanish, Zavala realized that he, as a federalist reformer, was being denied an opportunity to receive credit for any diplomatic success. This was not mere paranoia. By early 1834, Santa Anna had concluded that the Mexican people were not ready for the federalist reforms already in place and he embraced centralism. He publicly criticized Acting President Gómez Farías and arrived in Mexico City to take charge himself on April 24. Within a few days he told Congress to disband its current session or he would dismiss the members.

Federalists objected strenuously, but Santa Anna told them that the vice president and the "hoodlum" Congress were tyrannizing the people. Gómez Farías immediately left the capital for his home in Zacatecas. Centralist newspapers crowed that "like an ill-fated comet" Gómez Farías had attracted "cholera and misery; immorality and tyranny . . . ignorance and sacrilege . . . the triumph of the worthless . . . and the debasement of the select people . . . ." The towns of Puebla, Jalapa, Orizaba, and Oaxaca, the president's strongholds, called on Santa Anna to take control, annul the reforms, and act in his own right until a new Congress could be selected.

Santa Anna accepted the invitation to assume dictatorial powers, but as a matter of form, submitted his acts to his hand-picked new centralist cabinet and Congress. Federalist states that objected to the unconstitutional acts received immediate punishment when centralist Santa Anna dismissed their legislatures. Santa Anna also restored the powers of the Church and the military, thereby consolidating his support.

Meanwhile in Paris, Zavala for a time became closely associated with his former political enemy, Anastasio Bustamante, the refugee centralist ex-president. Between June and August the pair met often for dinner, and Zavala's private secretary, Joaquín Moreno, believed they were discussing ways to save the Mexican republic. Their association continued until Zavala left Paris for the United States in early 1835.

Zavala resumed writing in Paris. He prepared a report in French about the ancient Mayan ruins at Uxmal and read it to the Royal Academy. That distinguished body honored him by making him a member. The discourse was published in *Antiquités Mexicaines* by his friend, H. Baradére, who would soon become interested in Texas.

Zavala also readied his 1830 travel journal for publication as *Viage a los Estados-Unidos del Norte de America*. During the summer when he realized that Santa Anna was destroying the federal republic, the book became more than just a travel account. In his concluding chapter he explained how he admired the stability of the United States and its lack of revolutions. He attributed this to two factors lacking in Mexico: widespread ownership of land and the personal freedoms guaranteed in the U.S. Constitution's Bill of Rights. Moreover, no favoritism was shown one class of people over another. Nowhere were individual rights more respected than in the United States where everyone participated in government. This situation attracted immigrants, and as a result, the economy prospered. "The people . . . are wise, economical and fond of accumulating capital for the future." One assumes that Zavala viewed his countrymen in opposite terms!

In *Viage*, written in Spanish for distribution in Mexico,

Zavala urged Mexicans to study and understand their northern neighbor as a way to improve their own country. In closing he enunciated his new philosophy, one that was bound to offend his countrymen: the southern states surrounding Mexico City were still dominated by the military and ecclesiastic hierarchy inherited from Spanish forefathers; there ignorance and prejudice against new ideas prevailed. At the same time, the less-populated states on the northern frontier from California and New Mexico to those bordering the Rio Grande were welcoming hard-working republic-minded emigrants from the United States and Europe. Besides the border states, Zavala listed Sonora, Sinoloa, Durángo, Chihuahua, Zacatecas, and San Luís Potosí as progressive and open to innovation. The newcomers brought their love of political democracy and their dislike of a state church and a powerful military. Thus northern Mexico would prosper while the states in the south would stagnate. When liberty triumphed in the north, wrote Zavala, it could spread southward with sufficient effort and education.

By the end of August, Zavala decided he could no longer represent a government that embraced centralism and aligned itself with the ecclesiastic and military elites. He resigned as Mexican minister to France on August 30, 1834. In a private letter to Santa Anna he vehemently denounced the president for abandoning the federalists who had brought him to office. He condemned him for his opportunistic policies and the dissolution of the legislative bodies. Still hoping to steer Santa Anna toward reform, Zavala urged him to avoid advice from churchmen and generals who used exclusion, privilege, and brute force to obtain their goals. The idealistic optimist exhorted Santa Anna to follow constitutional principles and call a national convention to reorganize the government; Zavala believed the 1824 Constitution was based on faulty illusions about creating a republic in Mexico.

Zavala's letters to the secretary of foreign relations and Santa Anna caused a furor in Mexico City. His emotional denunciation and condescending recommendations, so typical of Zavala when his principles were challenged, sealed his political fate. Acknowledging the receipt of Zavala's resignation, the foreign secretary warned that Santa Anna was greatly displeased by Zavala's criticism. Barely controlling his anger, the president wrote a terse letter to King Louis Philippe saying that he was recalling Zavala in order to employ him in a "position more advantageous to Mexico."

Zavala was to remain in Paris until his replacement arrived, but he sent his family to New York immediately. Perhaps this was to save expenses in Paris since his resignation implied the end of his salary, or maybe he was concerned for their safety. Another scenario may have included a hysterical wife. How well did Emily accept his resignation? She had been elevated in society as the wife of the governor of Mexico and then presented at the French court; now she had to return to New York as a nobody with her trunk of elegant clothes. No doubt the young woman was greatly disappointed. Zavala accompanied Emily and the children to Le Havre in September; Lorenzo, Jr., who had served as undersecretary at the Mexican ministry, would escort them to New York.

Zavala continued writing after his family left Paris. Besides a few articles, he started work on the third volume of his *Ensayo Histórico*. Unfortunately, the manuscript disappeared before it could be published. As an indication of the slant of his narrative, Bustamante asked him, probably unsuccessfully, to delete portions detrimental to the former acting president's reputation. Bustamante wanted to suppress details about the assassination of Guerrero in 1831 and the sensational 1832 suicide of Commandant General Manuel Mier y Terán, both of which happened during his administration.

Zavala's replacement arrived in Paris on February 27, 1835, and was presented at court by Zavala three weeks later. The Yucatecan took formal leave of the king on March 25. Louis Philippe issued what was probably the usual notice of departure sent to a diplomat's home government: "The personal qualities and the honorable conduct, which he has had during the whole period of his mission, have merited our esteem and our confidence."

Zavala left Paris at the end of March and sailed from Le Havre April 3. His six-month service as Mexican minister plenipotentiary had been both enjoyable and frustrating for the increasingly complex man. Being in Paris, meeting powerful and interesting people, and visiting cultural and historic places stimulated Zavala, the intellectual. Zavala, the politician, enjoyed the challenge of intricate international diplomacy but was frustrated by his inability to move Mexican officials toward diplomatic goals, especially Spanish recognition of Mexican independence. Zavala, the federalist, wondered if he had a political future in Mexico while Zavala, the family man, worried about how he would support his growing family. Emily had written that she was expecting another child in May. Once again, just as in 1830, his financial well-being seemed to depend on those timely Texas land speculations.

The month-long crossing provided time for thought. Zavala had assured Mexican officials that he would be returning to Mexico City as ordered, but he sensed that he would become a political prisoner or worse. Instead he would go to Texas to see about his speculative land. He could also visit the federalist refugees in New Orleans—Mexía was there since Santa Anna banished him in August.

Perhaps the Mexican refugees would consider Zavala's new idea that the north Mexican federalist states should become a new nation allied commercially or even politically with Louisiana. The Crescent City had always been a seedbed of political plotting, and such a rumor was current there. There were many options—maybe a revolution to remove Santa Anna from power would answer federalist needs. Alternative ideas, almost as numerous as the waves on the ocean, filled the head of the ambitious man heading for New York.

CHAPTER *6*

Zavala and the State of Texas, 1835

ZAVALA landed in New York City on May 4, 1835, and five days later wrote to Joel Poinsett that he was going to Texas to encourage its separation from Mexico. He did this not for independence for its own sake, but to encourage the formation of a north Mexican federation. He told Poinsett that it was "impossible for the South of the Mexican Republic to remain united to the North where there is a new population, full of life and receiving reinforcements from the United States." He referred Poinsett to his new book, *Viage a los Estados Unidos*, for more details.

Zavala also told the secretary of foreign relations and General Miguel Barragán, Santa Anna's new vice president and currently acting president, that he intended to make his home in Texas. He explained that he wanted to remain aloof from the partisan politics that threatened Mexico, and, more importantly, he needed to restore his personal finances, depleted by his long service in public office. The centralists in Mexico City knew him too well to believe that he could remove himself from politics. The secretary of foreign relations issued a letter on June 6 ordering Zavala to return to Veracruz and sent copies to appropriate Mexican officials along the gulf coast and in Texas.

Mexico was in turmoil. At Santa Anna's urging, Congress had reduced the state militias to one militiaman for every 500 inhabitants, a step intended to destroy pockets of federalism. Zacatecas, the home of former Vice President Gómez Farías and strongly federalist in politics, refused to decrease its militia. President Santa Anna personally led 3,500 troops northward in April to punish the recalcitrant state. An order to arrest Gómez Farías forced the ardent federalist and his family into hiding. They tried to flee to Texas but could not avoid patrols looking for them; finally they managed to reach Matamoros where they sailed to exile in New Orleans on August 15. Santa Anna quickly defeated the 5,000 Zacatecas militiamen and turned his victorious soldiers loose to rape, pillage, and burn in the state capital. Resident foreigners were special targets.

Coahuila-Texas legislators meeting in Monclova, over 300 miles north of Zacatecas, believed they would be the next victims. The federalist governor, Agustín Viesca, awarded ten-league grants in Texas to prominent Anglos who could raise money, arms, and men to defend the state. Disappointed speculators who did not receive one of the large tracts returned to Texas to arouse public opinion against the supposed "Mammoth Speculation." At the end of May, the legislators and Governor Viesca fled Monclova toward San Antonio, intending to relocate the state capital. A few escaped, but most were arrested on orders of the commandant general of northeastern Mexico, Martín Perfecto de Cós, Santa Anna's brother-in-law.

In May, Santa Anna and most of the satiated troops turned south instead of north and Coahuila-Texas was spared. Santa Anna triumphantly marched into Mexico City and was named *benemérito en grado heroico*. His subservient Congress recessed without withdrawing his emergency rank of general-in-chief conferred for the Zacatecas campaign, thus allowing him to be both president and supreme military commander. As usual, Santa Anna retired to his estate, leaving Vice President Barragán in charge of day-to-day concerns.

Zavala remained in New York for Ricardo's birth on May 26 and his baptism by Father Varela on June 2. During May, Lorenzo, Jr., started to Texas to see about his father's land and look for a possible home for the family. The young man and his Swiss servant, Joseph, traveled by stagecoach to the Ohio River, then by steamer to Natchez. There they boarded a small steamboat to ascend the Red River to Natchitoches, Louisiana, where they bought horses for the seventy-five-mile ride to Nacogdoches. On June 23 before the Nacogdoches *alcalde*, Lorenzo, Jr., filed his required character certificate, endorsed by a leading Anglo resident, to become a citizen and apply for land in Texas. The pair turned south and traveled through the forested wilderness to John Bevil's settlement near present-day Jasper. They doubtless visited the newly appointed special land commissioner for the Zavala grant, George W. Smyth. From there they followed Indian trails through the dense forests and grassy plains, reaching upper Galveston Bay and the San Jacinto estuary in late July.

Zavala, Sr., left for Texas immediately after Ricardo's baptism and followed his son's route except that he bypassed Natchez to reach New Orleans on July 3. No records document what he did for the next four days, but he must have visited Mexía and the federalist sympathizers, most of whom were Masons. There was much to discuss although Gómez Farías had not yet arrived to express his views. New Orleans had heard about the attack on Zacatecas, but of more immediate concern for local merchants was the seizure of United States vessels by a Mexican cruiser visiting Texas ports.

Zavala arranged for passage to the Brazos River on the schooner *San Felipe*. It was the only vessel sailing regularly between New Orleans and the Brazos River. That was because Thomas F. McKinney, the senior partner of the McKinney and Williams commission house at Quintana at the mouth of the river, was a major investor in the vessel. Mexía, who knew McKinney, probably suggested the schooner and supplied his friend with a letter of introduction to McKinney. Zavala boarded on July 7 and cleared the mouth of the Mississippi the following day.

A veteran mariner, Captain William A. Hurd no doubt had instructions from McKinney to arm the vessel in New Orleans for this voyage. McKinney and Hurd were determined that this schooner would resist seizure by Mexican patrol boats cruising the Texas coast. McKinney had been on board his schooner *Columbia* on May 9 when the Mexican cruiser *Montezuma* seized it near the mouth of the Brazos. Captain Juan Calvi released the passengers but took both the vessel and its "contraband" cargo and another vessel, the *Martha*, to Matamoros. A man of action with a hot temper, McKinney angrily complained to Ramón Múzquiz, the political *jéfe* in San Antonio, that his vessel was under Mexican registry and was not carrying contraband. The New Orleans customs collector, prodded by merchants who lost cargoes, responded by sending his revenue cutter to patrol the Texas coast.

The *San Felipe* arrived safely at Quintana about July 12 to the relief of the captain, McKinney, and Zavala. Mexía would have almost certainly told Zavala that McKinney was a federalist sympathizer. He had met the Kentucky native when he visited the Brazos communities in July 1832. At that time Colonel Mexía, commanding federalist forces, had just captured Matamoros from President Bustamante's centralist troops. The victor, accompanied by Stephen F. Austin who happened to be there, sailed to Texas with five troop ships prepared to defeat a rumored Anglo Texan rebellion. The Texans explained that they had attacked the administration forts at Anahuac and Velasco acting as federalist supporters of Santa

Anna, not as rebels against Mexico. This was not exactly true but Mexía had chosen to believe it. Mexía had pleasant memories of the banquets and ceremonies held by the Texans in his honor.

McKinney was one of the most influential men in Texas at this time. In 1823 he had traveled the Santa Fe Trail from Missouri to Chihuahua and had returned to the United States by way of Texas. He settled first in Nacogdoches, where he had a store, but in 1830 he moved to the Brazos where he became a substantial commission merchant and a good friend of Stephen F. Austin.

Surprisingly, given his temperament, McKinney also got along well with many of those who disagreed with Austin's longtime policy of accommodating Mexican leaders. Since 1830, an increasing number of newcomers felt no loyalty toward the Mexican republic and wanted Texas annexed to the United States. Old-timers in Austin's colony who had benefited from the generous Mexican land grants tended to support Austin and were called the "peace party" by the newcomers such as William Barret Travis, Henry Smith, and William H. and John Wharton. These four and their adherents were known by 1835 as the "war party" because they urged strong steps to sever Texas from Mexico.

McKinney, busy with the seasonal cotton shipments, turned Zavala over to his friend, lawyer William H. Jack who had a plantation across the river near Velasco and another place near Columbia. Jack was a member of the committee of vigilance, correspondence, and safety recently organized at Columbia, the court town for the lower Brazos settlements. Zavala was surprised to learn the degree of unrest and uncertainty in Texas—nobody in New Orleans had prepared him for the situation, if indeed they knew about it when he left.

The Anglo Texans became alarmed in mid-June when word reached the Brazos about the arrest of Governor Agustín Viesca of Coahuila-Texas and the supposed gigantic land speculations. Amid rumors that additional troops were on their way to Texas, the overwrought and suspicious citizens seized a military courier riding from San Antonio to Anahuac. His dispatches confirmed the reports about more troops, and the hot-headed Travis started to Anahuac on June 22 with a few volunteers to capture the small garrison before it could be reinforced. There had been a recent confrontation at Anahuac between the citizens and the customs collector about unequal levies. Anglo emotions were easily stirred and some spoke of raising a force to capture the large garrison at San Antonio and also going to Coahuila to rescue the governor.

In typical American fashion, but contrary to Mexican law that did not provide the right to assemble, the residents of San Felipe and Columbia held meetings on June 22 and 23. These two villages were the largest in the Department of the Brazos, one being the departmental center and the other the *ayuntamiento* for the lower Brazos. At a second meeting at conservative Columbia on Sunday, June 28, resolutions were adopted urging moderation, adherence to the federal constitution, and preparedness. Stephen F. Austin's sister and her husband, James F. Perry, lived nearby, and, like many in the immediate area, supported the peace party.

About the time Zavala arrived at Quintana, Travis returned to San Felipe from Anahuac with the forty Mexican soldiers and the commander, Captain Antonio Tenorio. Travis was surprised that the peace party had stirred up a great deal of criticism of his expedition, and he finally asked in the newspaper that the public suspend its condemnations until he could explain.

Leaders in Columbia and San Felipe feared that Travis' precipitous attack would cause military retaliation from San Antonio. They called a conference of representatives from all the communities within the Brazos district to meet in San Felipe on July 15. William H. Jack asked James B. Miller, the political chief for the Department of the Brazos, to invite Zavala to the meeting.

Accompanied by Peter Bertram of Brazoria and Wade H. Bynum of Velasco, "General" Zavala rode north to Columbia where he met with the local vigilance committee before going to San Felipe. Zavala asked what the local people thought about declaring Texas independent from Mexico. This innocent query made the members wary. Not knowing what his intentions were, the committee's response was cold.

Somewhat disappointed by his reception, Zavala and his escort returned to Velasco the next morning, apparently to talk with William Jack, instead of continuing to San Felipe as they had planned. Two days later Zavala returned to Columbia where he spent the night. One member of the cautious committee wrote, "What he intends I do not know—the Americans want no Mexicans to hear them.... There are various reports suspecting his intentions." Some believed that he had come to settle on his land and "knew nothing of our confusion until he arrived here." Others thought that "he has been put up to aiding and assisting in our Independence...." The writer, one William H. Sledge of Columbia, concluded that in the end, "we must depend on ourselves and not upon an aspiring Mexican." He added that those residents who previously "were so hot for war" now said nothing.

This letter, brimming with ethnic prejudice, represented the common Anglo Texan racial attitude toward Mexicans in 1835; additionally there was the universal frontier suspicion about foreigners and strangers. Zavala's experiences in the more cosmopolitan East Coast seaports and New Orleans did not prepare him for the ethnic snobbery of less sophisticated men living along the Brazos. These people did not want his advice and questioned his motives. Few in Texas knew, or even wanted to know, anything about his political experience. Within a few days, however, three war party men from San Felipe—Robert M. Williamson, Frank W. Johnson, and Joseph Baker—called on him in Columbia. One peace party Texan believed the four were probably conspiring against the Mexican authorities.

Zavala's arrival on the Brazos quickly became known to the Mexican authorities in San Antonio. As soon as Captain Tenorio heard that Zavala was visiting at Velasco, he wrote to Colonel Ugartechea, the commandant in San Antonio. Ugartechea could sympathize with Tenorio's plight as a "guest" of the Texans. In June 1832 he himself had been forced to surrender the fort at Velasco to the Anglo Texans and even spent some time at San Felipe. The same mail pouch heading to San Antonio with Tenorio's reports also contained letters to Ugartechea from the Brazos political chief and other leaders professing their loyalty and their regrets about Travis' action.

Meanwhile, Captain Tenorio on June 24 received an order dated ten days earlier from Commandant General Cós at Matamoros instructing all military commanders to arrest Zavala and send him to Veracruz should he appear in their jurisdictions. Also included in the arrest order was one for "Ex-general Mexía," rumored to be in Texas. Tenorio immediately asked the political chief in San Felipe for assistance in arresting Zavala, but Miller replied that *he* had received no orders to arrest Zavala. Thus began a long game of officially acknowledging orders to seize Zavala while making excuses why the orders could not be executed. Even Ugartechea, who was considered pro-federalist by some of his superiors, delayed. When he received the message from Tenorio on July 25, he told Commandant General Cós that he could not make the arrest because he lacked sufficient troops. The Yucatán federalist had now gained sympathy and protection from many Anglo Texans who could not believe that the military had the authority to arrest civilians.

Before the end of July, Zavala met his son near Harrisburg on Buffalo Bayou where Lorenzo, Jr., had found a comfortable house for the family. The nearby San Jacinto River where Zavala owned five leagues was on the eastern edge of Austin's colony and was part of the Department of the Brazos. Philip Singleton wanted to sell his one-story home, probably board and batten over logs (there had been two sawmills in the area for some time), which sat on a high peninsula over-looking Buffalo Bayou. The house was near the bayou's junction with the San Jacinto River, a scenic and convenient site with easy access to Galveston Bay. Zavala sensed the commercial advantage of the area and willingly paid seven dollars an acre, a total of $1,239, for the 177-acre tract including the home, a smaller house, and outbuildings.

Zavala liked the location and the neighborhood better than the heavily forested Brazos communities. Here the tree-lined banks gave way to open prairies and long vistas of open water leading to the Gulf. A number of solid citizens lived around the San Jacinto estuary including David G. Burnet. He had come in 1831 soon after selling his empresario grant to the Galveston Bay Company and had a home and a sawmill on the eastern shore near Nathaniel Lynch's ferry and tavern. William Scott, the wealthy father-in-law of Austin's former assistant, Samuel May Williams, now McKinney's mercantile partner, lived south of the Lynch complex near Goose Creek.

On the western shore were the Cloppers, former Ohio residents who had come in 1828 as merchants. They had owned the large peninsula jutting into the estuary, but had sold it recently to James Morgan whose name became attached to the promontory. Morgan was the Texas agent for several New York land speculators including Samuel Swartwout, the collector of the Port of New York, and James Treat, the Mexican vice consul. Zavala knew both men and was delighted to learn that the New Washington Association planned a town on Morgan's Point. Morgan was currently in New York and expected to return in November with two vessels and artisans to build the town. This was exactly the commercial enterprise so admired by Zavala. He immediately sent a letter to New York so that his family could travel to Texas with Morgan.

The orders and evasions concerning Zavala's arrest now expanded to include a number of Anglo Texans who had offended Mexican centralists—Travis, Johnson, Baker,

Williamson, and Samuel May Williams, continued into September. Meanwhile a series of meetings took place in the various communities. Zavala was living temporarily at Sloop Point, the home of Andrew Clopper adjacent to Morgan's Point, while the Singletons moved out of the house. His neighbors asked him to speak at the meeting planned for August 8 at Lynch's tavern. This was what he had hoped for, but he declined because he was ill. He began suffering with intermittent fever (malaria) while in the Brazos communities, and the chills, fever, and rheumatic pains continued on the San Jacinto where a number of residents had the same malady. A seasoned traveler and cognizant of the tropical climate, Zavala carried a small supply of remedies in his medicine chest and doctored himself.

In spite of his illness, Zavala wrote a clear summary of the political situation to be read at the meeting at Lynchburg. Sensing that talk about independence was premature, he focused on arousing sentiment to remove Santa Anna. The president, Zavala explained, had come into office pretending to be the defender of the 1824 Constitution but soon destroyed it. He dissolved Congress, banished Vice President Gómez Farías, destroyed the civic militias, and recently closed the state legislatures. As a student of the United States Constitution and American history, Zavala knew that these issues would anger the Anglo Americans.

Such acts, he said, nullified obedience from the people since the fundamental compact (the words of John Locke, one of Zavala's favorite authors) had been broken. Because the compact was destroyed, the states must act for their own best interests. In the case of Coahuila-Texas, General Cós used the sale of the land as a pretext to arrest the governor, threaten the legislators, and impose military rule. Texas, however, was still relatively free of troops and the people should immediately organize to restore harmony and order. Zavala recommended that a representative convention meet in mid-October, giving the neighborhoods time to select delegates.

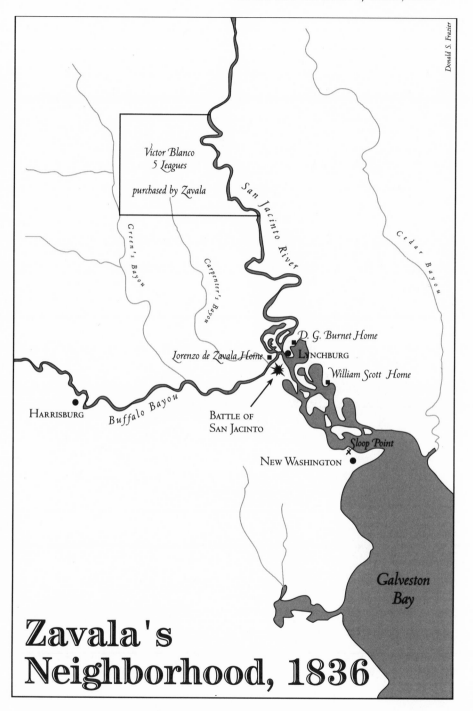

Donald S. Frazier

Victor Blanco
5 Leagues

purchased by Zavala

San Jacinto River

Cedar Bayou

Green's Bayou

Carpenter's Bayou

D. G. Burnet Home

Lorenzo de Zavala Home

Lynchburg

William Scott Home

Harrisburg

Buffalo Bayou

Battle of
San Jacinto

Sloop Point

New Washington

Galveston
Bay

Zavala's
Neighborhood, 1836

As an afterthought, Zavala added that Mexican officials would demand obedience from the Texans because of the generous land grants made to settlers, but they should resist. It was the liberals—such as himself, not the centralists now in power—who arranged the land grants for immigrants and were now being persecuted by the centralist administration.

Zavala's neighbors elected William Scott to preside. He named Burnet, the only man present who had legal training, to chair a five-man committee to draft resolutions. The eleven articles reflected Burnet's conservative views and his own agenda at this time. Burnet hoped for an appointment as superior judge or even governor of Texas and therefore favored appeasement. Burnet overawed his neighbors with rhetoric, and his measures passed. Had Zavala been present, he might have defeated the verbose opportunist.

While Burnet agreed that Santa Anna had violated the rights of the people, he passed no judgement on his future government. He trusted Mexican leaders to organize a government "with the spirit of the 19th century. . . based on wise and equitable laws" to guarantee the individual political liberty. However, the national government should not blame land speculators for the current disturbance in Texas; if any wrong was done, the law could correct it. Finally, delegates attending the proposed October meeting should preserve the peace in Texas and the unity of the Mexican nation.

Those attending the meeting chose Burnet and David B. Macomb, a former officer in the United States army, to be delegates to the planned consultation. Burnet hurried to Brazoria to place the San Jacinto resolutions in the weekly *Texas Republican*, the only newspaper in Texas at this time, once owned by and still influenced by William H. Wharton. The editor, F. C. Gray, leaned more toward the war party and would not predict when he could print Burnet's offering because he was inundated with material for the next issue. Outraged, Burnet left with his manuscript.

Doubtless disappointed with the San Jacinto resolutions,

Zavala soon learned that the lower Brazos communities had come alive. The day after the San Jacinto meeting, ninety-two men representing both factions gathered at Brazoria and signed a petition calling for a convention. The list included the Wharton brothers, McKinney, and editor Gray of the *Republican*. A week later on August 15, William H. Wharton chaired a meeting at Columbia that endorsed the "Consultation" of all Texas and urged the reorganization of the local committee of safety to better represent the municipality and to defend "our rights." The seven resolutions adopted included a promise not to "give up any individual to the Military authorities," while another authorized publication of the proceedings in the *Texas Republican*. The new vigilance committee chaired by Wharton's friend, Branch T. Archer, endorsed the calling of the Consultation. The thirteen men who signed the circular were mostly war party in philosophy and included John A. Wharton, Henry Smith, and Zavala's friends, William H. Jack, Peter Bertram, and W. H. Bynum.

When the citizens of San Felipe met on August 26, two of William Jack's brothers took an active part. Those attending endorsed the Columbia resolutions and the call for the Consultation. Travis took heart and wrote to Burnet on August 31, enclosing copies of the Columbia and San Felipe resolutions. "We" are sworn to "support a federal republican govt. not a military usurpation...the people are becoming united....I hope you are with us." Obviously he had not seen Burnet's San Jacinto resolutions. Travis wrote to friends in Harrisburg and Anahuac that the "Mexican or Tory party" was "routed horse and foot." It was the tories, he said, who had denounced the war party leaders to the authorities, resulting in the orders for their arrest. Their trials would have been before a military court in San Antonio, which was "too much for the people to bear." Zavala's Harrisburg neighbors let him read Travis' letter.

The war party received firm support on September 1 when Stephen F. Austin returned to Texas. His long stay in Mexico

City had changed his policy from accommodation to confrontation. When he reached New Orleans from Veracruz on August 11, he no longer trusted the federalists. He wrote to his cousin and Samuel May Williams, Austin's lieutenant, both in the United States, urging an increase in immigration to Texas. "She must rely upon herself, and . . . needs strength" of "efficient and active and intelligent men. . . ."

Texans welcomed Austin after his sixteen-month absence with a banquet and ball at Brazoria on September 8. Austin endorsed the proposed Consultation and four days later presided at a meeting in San Felipe that endorsed adherence to the 1824 Mexican Constitution. Within a week Brazos residents learned that General Cós was expected in San Antonio on September 18 and would then march eastward. Austin issued a circular urging unity and preparedness; each district should mobilize its militia in case of need. All conciliatory measures had failed, said Austin, and "war is our only recourse." As late as September 14, Austin expected San Antonio federalists to join them, but with Cós occupying San Antonio, that hope dimmed.

Meanwhile, Zavala, recovering from his recent fever, received a copy of Austin's September 8 banquet speech. Writing from "Linchburg" on September 17, he praised Austin's effort, saying that it should unite the Texans. The Yucatecan believed that the Anglos "will defend their private rights until death; but still do not realize the necessity for cooperation." Zavala offered some prophetic observations: delegates to the Consultation would be confused; few had any legislative experience. To whom will they direct their decisions? Who will execute the decisions? Worse, two parties would form: one will say they have the power to create a new republic and demand independence. The other faction would "Consult," draft a few reports, and adjourn. Zavala added, ". . . both parties are dangerous and . . . the second is mortal."

Zavala, now hoping to reform Mexico and perhaps dreaming of the presidency, warned Austin that "*absolute*" independence should not be discussed. Instead, delegates should draft resolutions saying that as a state in the Mexican Federation, Texas would defend its rights under the social contract. It should offer asylum to persecuted Mexicans and join the Mexican confederation as a free and independent state if and when the states recovered their lost rights. If Mexico did not recover, then Texas should take independent action.

At the same time, Zavala advised Austin not to support the flawed Constitution of 1824. Instead, Texas should "support the federal bases of the Constitution and nothing more." As for Santa Anna, he was doomed to failure. He had only limited troops and the support of the priests and a few undependable rich men. An uprising anywhere would cause him trouble, but "Texas is his certain death." If he comes himself, the refugee predicted, it will be fatal. "The rivers, forest, deserts, rifles . . . and the American steadfastness" will bring him to a quick end.

While the Texans made plans to resist General Cós, Zavala's federalist friends in New Orleans met on September 3 and 4 to plan the defeat of Santa Anna. Former Vice President Gómez Farías and his family had arrived in the Crescent City on August 29, four days after Austin left for Texas. Mexía and the others welcomed him and organized a meeting of the Amphictyonic Council for September 3. The name came from ancient Greece: amphictyons (deputies) represented their neighborhoods at meetings of a league of states at Delphi or Thermopylae. The New Orleans group included both Mexican federalists and Anglo Americans who were united by commercial interests and freemasonry. Mexía outlined a plan to attack Tampico and rally federalists to attack Santa Anna. He already had tentative financial backing from some Louisiana capitalists, provided he could guarantee the sale of Texas to the Louisiana interests. Texas would be made an independent state, temporarily under the guidance of the United States, until "a new republic of the South" could be organized that included the north Mexican states.

Gómez Farías thought the plan impractical and did not like the idea of severing Texas even temporarily, saying that the Mexican people would not understand. He recommended that Mexía's proposed invasion be postponed. But the supporters of the scheme argued the invasion was in the interest of all liberals, which brought Gómez Farías reluctantly into the fold.

The meeting on September 4 debated the issues of bringing "true liberty" to the United States of Mexico. A two-thirds majority approved seven articles: Gómez Farías, Mexía, and Zavala would lead the effort to return the federal system and liberalism to Mexico. Gómez Farías was the nominal head while Mexía, as head of the Federal army, was to recruit men in Louisiana and later the civic militia of Tamaulipas and other Mexican states. Zavala would direct the Texans in an uprising to draw attention and Santa Anna's army away from Mexía's landing at Tampico. Amnesty would be offered to all except Santa Anna and his ministers, who would be executed. Mexía would petition Congress to reform the 1824 Constitution by restricting the power of the clergy and the military, while freedom of religion would be established along with land reform. United States citizens, as a reward for their support, could enter Mexico without passports and be exempt from one-third of the import duties. Thirty-seven men signed the document, but their names did not appear in the December newspaper article published in Mexico City, the only known record of this meeting. Seemingly the Amphictyons had a spy in their midst.

Zavala and Mexía must have discussed the plan in July, because the wording used some of Zavala's phrases. Moreover, his questions to the Columbia committee about support for independence fit the scheme. There was sufficient time for Zavala to tell Mexía about his cool reception, but perhaps Mexía and even Zavala believed that the Texans would rally in time.

Meanwhile events in Texas came to a head. Residents of the Brazos learned on September 19 that General Cós was landing 400 men and cannon at Copano Bay, the port serving Goliad and San Antonio. Reliable information indicated that Cós, after settling at San Antonio, intended to march to the Brazos even if the wanted Texans were surrendered. Austin quickly wrote letters to all communities asking volunteers to meet on the Lavaca River to intercept the soldiers. On September 21 Austin sent express riders to Harrisburg, Nacogdoches, and the communities north of San Felipe asking for militiamen (all male residents over age seventeen) and volunteers. He also asked Zavala to join him in San Felipe as quickly as possible.

Austin's message reached Harrisburg two days later, and local leaders immediately sent copies to "General Zavala," Lynchburg, Liberty, and Bevil's settlement. They assured Austin that some of the Harrisburg militia would leave on the 26th for the rendezvous while the neighbors would "assist the Govr. on his way to Sanfellipe . . . . All to a man in this quarter are preparing for the defense of their county against military tyrany [sic] and despotism. Texas and Liberty is the motto."

By September 30 Zavala had joined Austin in Sam Williams' vacant country residence on a ten-acre tract outside of San Felipe. Although the house was unfurnished, the two had quiet, ample space with "private rooms to write in." Austin expected a few others would join them to help in "the formation of a govt. (perhaps of a nation). . . ." He asked his brother-in-law near Quintana to send furniture, bedding, other household goods, food and wine, plus a servant to San Felipe on the *Laura* so that they would be more comfortable.

Just as Zavala and Austin were settling into their "bachellors hall" at San Felipe, the citizens of Gonzales were moving their families out of town. Colonel Ugartechea had sent a cavalry company from San Antonio to recover a cannon loaned to the residents four years earlier for defense against Indian attacks. Local men refused to surrender the small cannon, and on October 2, reinforced by volunteers, the Texans defeated Ugartechea's troops and forced them back to San Antonio. The war had begun and the Anglos expected retaliation from Cós.

During this crisis, Zavala contributed to the October 3 circular addressed to the "People" that was prepared by Austin, chair of the central committee of safety. The long exposition detailed conditions in Texas and Mexico that led to calling out the militia on September 19. In this essay, Austin made clear his respect for Zavala, the man General Cós had "particularly designated and aimed at" for arrest. Zavala had come to Texas seeking asylum from persecution, said Austin. "His offense we know not, except that he is the known friend of free institutions." Cós had ordered Colonel Ugartechea to march into the colony and take this "distinguished man" prisoner no matter the cost. However, the threats against "this patriotic and virtuous citizen" outraged the civil authorities of Texas, who found ways to protect him.

Zavala briefly visited his home the first week in October but returned to San Felipe by October 15, the day the Consultation was to begin. He was again suffering intermittent fever but was pleased to have been chosen one of five Harrisburg delegates. Burnet had been passed over because of his August 8 toryish resolutions. He had secured nomination as a deputy from Liberty, but he failed to attend. So many of the elected representatives decided to join the volunteer army at Gonzales that Zavala and those remaining at San Felipe postponed the opening session until November.

On October 8, Austin had gone to Gonzales where the volunteers elected him their commanding officer. The remaining three members of the central committee asked delegates to the Consultation to join them if unable to go to the army. Zavala thus became a member of what was called the Permanent Council; between October 17 and 31, the membership changed often and attendance fluctuated, once reaching a maximum of twenty-four.

The members of the Permanent Council named Zavala to the finance committee and urged him to write an article for Mexican Texans about recent events. His essay appeared in San Felipe's newly established *The Telegraph and Texas Register* on October 31. What influence it had is difficult to assess. Political leaders in San Antonio, naturally cautious frontiersmen, also had reservations about the Yucatecan and his land speculations in Texas.

The Consultation reached a quorum on November 3, and Chairman Branch T. Archer of Brazoria named Zavala to represent Harrisburg on the "committee of twelve." It was composed of one delegate from each municipality; the members would write a declaration "setting forth to the world the causes that impelled us to take up arms, and the objects for which we fight." Other members among this distinguished dozen included John A. Wharton, chair, Richard R. Royal, R. M. Williamson, all of whom Zavala had known previously, and Sam Houston. As Zavala had predicted earlier, two groups vied to control both the committee and the entire membership of the Consultation—one favoring independence and the other for reform within the Mexican nation. Zavala was often the peacemaker between the factions. His personal preference for remaining within the Republic of Mexico and reforming the Constitution of 1824 ultimately won endorsement by the delegates.

After three days of argument and concession, the members voted thirty-three to fourteen on November 6 to create a provisional state government "based on the principles of the constitution of 1824." A second vote took place immediately: "All in favor of independence" resulted in fifteen for and thirty-three against. The committee of twelve returned to work on a formal declaration and the organization of a state government.

The declaration was approved the next day and 1,000

copies were ordered from the printer. Zavala volunteered to translate the declaration into Spanish, and the members approved 500 more copies in that language for distribution in San Antonio and elsewhere. Sensitive to Anglo feelings, Zavala asked that he not be referred to as "Governor Zavala" in the records, and a colleague proposed that all such titles be stricken from members' names.

Meanwhile, an agent from the New Orleans committee brought sixty-five volunteers to Brazoria. He hurried to San Felipe to tell Zavala and the others that fifty more armed men were on their way to Texas by way of Nacogdoches while General Mexía was sailing to Tampico with 150 men. The agent brought a letter from Mexía to McKinney detailing the plan, which Zavala translated into English. A select committee of six including Zavala reported Mexía's diversionary undertaking, along with other military matters, on November 13.

The members created a provisional state government before adjourning on November 14. They chose Henry Smith, a xenophobic member of the war party who favored independence, as governor and James W. Robinson, a moderate, lieutenant governor. Robinson would preside over the council composed of one member from each of the fourteen municipalities present. A lack of clear instructions defining executive and legislative authority set the stage for bitter conflict. The six-member Harrisburg delegation chose William P. Harris, brother of Harrisburg's founder, to represent the neighborhood.

Zavala probably had mixed emotions at the close of the Consultation. He had worked hard to keep the independence party from achieving its goal, yet the Consultation chose Henry Smith governor, a man who did not conceal his contempt for Mexicans. Zavala's dream of restoring federalism in Mexico, and even the Amphictyonic Council's scheme to forge a new nation with the north Mexican states, seemed doomed.

Zavala left San Felipe before learning about the rude reception given to Governor Agustín Viesca of Coahuila-Texas. Arrested and removed from office by General Cós, Viesca escaped from prison with federalist aid. Escorted by thirty men, he fled to Texas expecting to resume his office. When he reached Goliad on November 11, the Anglo commander refused to recognize him. At San Felipe, newly elected Governor Smith turned away the federalist volunteers and would not receive Viesca. In December, discouraged and uneasy, Viesca started toward Nacogdoches on his way to New Orleans where he would be safer.

Zavala's hopes now rested with Mexía's Tampico expedition. The scheme won support during the October 13 meeting in New Orleans where federalists and Texan sympathizers joined to raise money and recruits to defeat Santa Anna's troops in Texas. Lorenzo, Jr., was probably in attendance, having arrived in the city at the end of September. Mexía and about 150 volunteers, mostly Anglo Americans, left on November 6 and reached their destination eight days later. Bad luck plagued their landing. Prearranged federalist support failed to appear in sufficient numbers because of centralist propaganda linking Mexía to the secession movement in Texas. In desperation Mexía's volunteers tried to land secretly at night, but the schooner went aground and broke apart. The men waded ashore, their weapons wet and their ammunition ruined. Thirty-five federalist volunteers joined them and supplied new ammunition in time for a midnight attack against the town. However, the centralist commandant and 300 men were waiting and killed eight volunteers and took thirty-one prisoners. The remainder, tired and out of ammunition, retreated to the harbor where they chartered a schooner to take them to Texas.

The vessel reached the mouth of the Brazos River on December 3, and Mexía sent a report to Governor Viesca assuming he was in charge. Discovering his error, he sent Governor Henry Smith a second account of the unlucky expedition. Mexía, without funds or provisions, asked for orders to send the survivors to Austin's volunteers in the field. Fortunately, a federalist captain arrived in San Felipe seeking the advice of Zavala and Viesca. He told sympathetic council members that many federalists in northern Mexico would cooperate with the Texans if assured they were fighting for the federal republic, not for independence. The council immediately ordered the army contractor to give Mexía's men all the assistance they needed to join Austin at San Antonio. Governor Smith, however, vetoed the measure, saying that he had no confidence in Mexía, and he opposed trusting Mexicans in any situation. The council overruled the governor the next day and some of Mexía's men started west.

Amid more contradictory orders, Mexía sent a dignified letter to Governor Smith on December 23 saying that since he had failed to receive a reply from the governor, he presumed that his services were not "desired or necessary." He planned to return to New Orleans and then join federalists in the interior of Mexico to oppose Santa Anna.

There is no evidence that Mexía and Zavala met or exchanged letters during this period of quarrels and confusion, but surely the former friends were in contact. Zavala must have been devastated by the failure of the Tampico expedition.

Moreover, Zavala worried about his family, on their way from New York. He wrote in his journal, "I spent the worst days of my life because of lack of news of my family." Emily and the children finally arrived in early December on board the schooner *Flash*. James Morgan, after watching the *Flash* and *Kosciusko* depart from New York about November 1, escorted Emily, the three youngest children (young Henry Cresswell de Zavala remained in New York to attend school), and her Irish maid to New Orleans by way of the Ohio and Mississippi rivers. They met the schooners at the mouth of the Mississippi where Morgan had a cannon and arms placed on board. Because of the danger from armed Mexican vessels, the two small schooners sailed for Galveston Bay accompanied by two large, armed brigs. As the *Flash* slowly made its way up the San Jacinto estuary, neighbors sent word to Zavala at his home ten miles above Morgan's Point. The eager husband and father hurried to meet his family as the schooner came to its anchorage in the river off Morgan's Point. Zavala paid Morgan $110.51 to transport the freight and three servants from New York on board the *Flash*.

As 1835 came to a close, Zavala was happy that his family was safely in Texas but the future was uncertain. The Texas volunteers had captured San Antonio in early December, and General Cós agreed to retreat to Matamoros and not take up arms again against the Texans. But everybody expected that Santa Anna would return in the late spring, seeking revenge to redeem the honor of Mexico and his brother-in-law.

Isolated from the Brazos communities, Zavala may not have noticed the increasing antipathy against Mexicans among some Anglo Texans. Austin, however, found prejudice increasing in mid-December as he prepared to go to the United States to seek money, arms, and volunteers for Texas. He wrote to McKinney,

> The ideas advocated, and circulated through the country last summer when Zavala was at your house . . . are extending rapidly amongst the people. Mexía's situation is very unpleasant—he has scarsely [sic] escaped insult. . . . I am denounced as a Mexican . . . merely for treating Viesca and Mexía . . . with common politeness.

So far there had been no outrages, but he feared some of the "patriots" might embarrass Texas.

The Zavalas spent a quiet holiday season among their neighbors. They settled comfortably into the simple house with its large sitting-dining room and three small bedrooms. A wide covered porch ran the length of the front facing Buffalo Bayou and caught the prevailing Gulf breeze, adding an outdoor living space. Emily unpacked the furniture and

The Zavala home at Buffalo Bayou — from a watercolor at the Center for American History, University of Texas at Austin.

household goods she brought from New York but kept the fine silver and the eighteen rolls of French satin wallpaper stored for future use. What city-bred Emily thought about her new pastoral home can only be imagined—no intimate family letters have survived.

Within a short time, Zavala and his son would be called to serve their new country.

CHAPTER 7

Zavala and the
Republic of Texas,
1836

By EARLY JANUARY most Texans believed that
independence from Mexico was the only choice. In New
Orleans that month, Stephen F. Austin asked for money to
defend Texas but found neither funds nor volunteers if Texas
remained a state in the Mexican Republic. On the other
hand, he wrote on January 7, there was "all the aid, and support we need to sustain our independence." Moreover, the
federalists in Mexico "have done nothing . . . to aid us" and
some were even then marching north with Santa Anna. On
the same day, Sam Houston, commander-in-chief of a nonex-
istent Texas army, wrote to a friend from Washington-on-the-
Brazos that "there is but one course left . . . an unequivocal
Declaration of Independence."

Zavala, the pragmatic politician, searched his conscience
and found that he could accept the new direction being taken
by his colleagues. He was economically and politically tied to
Texas at this time; besides, his federalist friends seemed inca-

pable of positive action against Santa Anna. Zavala believed that the Texas climate, geography, and people would defeat Santa Anna just as the Russians had forced Napoleon to retreat from Moscow in 1812.

Meanwhile, the provisional state government disintegrated. Governor Smith quarreled with the lieutenant governor and the council. The governor vetoed nearly every ordinance passed by the pro-federalist council, which, in turn, overrode his veto. The climax came in January when the council authorized an offensive expedition against Matamoros; the governor, against the proposal, dismissed the council. On January 11, the council deposed the governor and named the lieutenant governor acting executive. After January 17, the council could not secure a quorum, and the governing of Texas was left to Lieutenant Governor Robinson and an advisory council that was neither legal nor popular. Everyone was waiting for the convention called for March 1, where delegates could declare Texas independent and organize a new government.

Voters went to the polls on February 1 to choose delegates to the convention. Seventy-three men voted at Lynchburg including Zavala and his son; Zavala and Andrew Briscoe won the nomination with sixty-five and twenty-nine votes, respectively. When the total was tallied for the entire Harrisburg municipality, the communities on Oyster Creek and Spring Creek increased Zavala's lead to 115 and Briscoe's to eighty. That so many Anglos voted for Zavala is remarkable in a time when candidates did not campaign and few knew him personally. He must have voiced his support for independence among his neighbors who then spread the word throughout the municipality that this experienced politician would best represent their interests.

Zavala dedicated himself to his family and his writing during the chilly months of January and February. He supervised a thorough housecleaning with the aid of his three French-speaking hired men and also had them prepare a large garden to sustain the family. He continued to suffer intermittent chills and fever but resumed writing the third volume of his history of Mexico.

Zavala left home the last week in February on a small mule for Washington-on-the-Brazos where the convention would take place. He reached the raw village on February 28 after three days riding into a cold norther; it being a leap year, he could rest one day before the session began. Although he knew that the site had been chosen for political reasons, he was surprised that the convention would be held in such a dismal place. One well-defined street led travelers from the ferry landing on the west bank to a dozen or so cabins and shanties scattered around a clearing in the forest. There was one tavern with a single room about forty by twenty feet where thirty visitors and the innkeeper's family slept as best they could. Tree stumps dotted the streets and lots; overall, the place was much worse than San Felipe sixty miles downriver, which at least had two taverns, five stores, and twenty or thirty modest houses.

Forty-five of the sixty-two elected delegates met Tuesday morning, March 1, with everybody shivering. The unfinished building lacked doors or covered windows until somebody tacked cotton cloth over the openings. The chair named Zavala one of four members to verify credentials.

Zavala saw many familiar faces from the Consultation, but most were new men. Among them were José Antonio Navarro and Francisco Ruíz from San Antonio, and as neither spoke much English, they relied on Zavala to translate for them. By the end of the first week, the three Mexican delegates joined William Fairfax Gray in a rented carpenter shop where they had more privacy. Gray, a Virginia lawyer visiting Texas as agent for some land speculators, found the three fascinating and wanted to learn Spanish.

On March 2, George C. Childress, recently from Tennessee, read his draft of the Texas Declaration of Independence to the assembled delegates. The members unanimously approved it without corrections or amendments, which surprised some. The following day the members signed the document, a step that earned Zavala the hatred of his former countrymen.

To win support from Mexican Texans, the president of the convention named Zavala and Navarro to the committee drafting the constitution for the new republic. Zavala chaired the section on the powers of the executive branch. The committee labored for two weeks and was still amending the document during the last hours of the session. Zavala received assignments to other committees—defense, naval affairs, and flag design. Whatever Zavala's first flag design was, others added a rainbow and a five-pointed star rising over the western horizon with a six-pointed star descending. Finally the letters TEXAS were placed between the points of the five-pointed star.

Zavala and the others became worried when a gloomy letter dated March 3 arrived from Travis at the Alamo; it was delivered during breakfast on Sunday, March 6. The ruins of the old mission chapel had been used as a barracks by Cós' army during the November and December siege by the Texans. After Cós' departure, the Texans occupied it and tried to improve its defenses. Travis and the others had been under siege in the compound since February 22. When Travis' letter was received, many of the onlookers started for San Antonio, not suspecting that all at the Alamo had died that same morning.

Meanwhile, work continued on pressing matters concerning the defense of Texas and how to pay for it. The members' worst fears were realized on March 15 when an express rider brought letters from General Houston written March 11 and 13 near Gonzales announcing the fall of the Alamo. Ruíz and Navarro received a similar message from Juan Seguín who was with Houston. A few delegates, fearing that Santa Anna was already marching eastward, left the convention to rescue their families; others departed to stockpile arms, horses, and wagons for both the army and the refugees.

The remaining members worked feverishly all the next

day, March 16, to complete the constitution and create a provisional government. While they were at supper, an express rider brought word that 2,000 Mexican cavalrymen were at Gonzales, about 100 miles away as the crow flies. (Mexican reports reveal, however, that there were 100 horsemen and modest numbers of infantry and artillerymen in General Joaquín Ramírez y Sesma's command nearing Gonzales on March 12. They were headed for San Felipe but subsequently became mired in the mud from torrential rain.) The panic-stricken members reassembled in poorly lit rooms to finish their work before leaving for their homes. After midnight the constitution was finished and adopted and an ordinance organizing a provisional government read and approved. The election of officers followed in the early hours of March 17.

Zavala supported the selection of cabinet members Samuel B. Carson, Bailey Hardeman, Thomas Jefferson Rusk, Robert Potter, and David Thomas for secretaries of state, treasury, war, navy, and attorney general. But tired as he was, he was not pleased by his own unanimous election as vice president nor that of David G. Burnet as president. The latter had won by seven votes over the better qualified Carson, a former United States congressman from North Carolina.

After initially refusing, Zavala reluctantly accepted his post when the members persuaded him that it would create a favorable impression among Mexican federalists. His confidence in Burnet to unite the Texans was less. Burnet had not been chosen a delegate but had appeared in Washington during the second week. He came as a lawyer seeking a pardon for his client who had murdered his son-in-law near Anahuac. Burnet argued that because the provisional state government ceased to exist, the convention was the only body with even a semblance of jurisdiction to prevent officials at Liberty from hanging his client. The members agreed in principle but said there was not time to investigate and granted the man a reprieve until May 1. As soon as Burnet had arrived, some spoke of him as a candidate for the interim president because many felt that delegates should not elect themselves to high office. Zavala's roommate, Gray, supposed that Burnet was probably "an honest, good man," but the Virginian, a keen judge of men, doubted "his ability for such a station."

What the delegates did not know about Burnet was that before the February elections he had campaigned through the lower Trinity River neighborhoods against independence. When people asked his advice, he told them to keep quiet and take no part. He even brought a petition to Washington signed by the residents asking the convention not to declare independence. Finding that the declaration was already adopted and signed when he arrived, he pocketed the damaging document and quietly campaigned for president.

The new officers took their oaths at 4:00 A.M. Thursday, March 17. Before the session reassembled later that morning, Burnet composed a verbose inaugural address that he delivered to the impatient delegates. After signing their names to the new constitution, most left for home. Burnet remained one more day, issuing bombastic directives. He called on the residents of eastern Texas to "deafen your ears against all rumours" and instead rally "to the field then, my countrymen, to the standard of liberty, and defend your rights in a manner worthy of your sires and yourselves." A second proclamation the same day implored Texans to join the army to "keep our wives and children . . . secure from pollution." Burnet explained that while the government was moving immediately to Harrisburg, it was not because the enemy was near—it was for "the common good." His final exhortation rivaled playwright Richard B. Sheridan's Mrs. Malaprop for peculiar syntax: Citizens should "gird up the loins of our minds" and turn back "this impotent invader."

Zavala, Ruíz, and Navarro, with their servants, horses, and Zavala's mule, crossed the ferry to the east bank of the Brazos on Friday, March 18, and that night camped alongside the road. Zavala was unwell the next morning, so the entire group remained in camp. Sunday they reached Jared E. Groce's

Retreat, a recently developed plantation where Zavala parted from his new friends. The two San Antonio men were headed downriver to San Felipe where they expected to hear news about their refugee families.

Zavala, Burnet, and the cabinet now headed southeast paralleling Spring Creek in present-day Waller and Harris counties, traveling toward Harrisburg. Gray joined the officials for the long ride over the prairie, and as they neared their destination, Zavala pointed to a dense line of trees on the eastern horizon where lay the five leagues purchased from Victor Blanco. They reached Buffalo Bayou after dark on March 22 and crossed to Harrisburg on a small flatboat. Gray and the new officers of the Republic spent the night in the home of Mrs. Jane B. Harris, widow of the founder of Harrisburg.

Zavala and Burnet returned to their homes the next day, and after prospecting over the neighborhood for valuable land, Gray crossed the bayou to visit the vice president. Gray, one year older than his host, found the house "beautifully situated" and the family interesting. Emily was a "fine, beautiful woman" with black eyes, a "tall, dignified person" with "ladylike manners." She maintained the household with an Irish maid and a black cook while the three French workmen cared for the garden and livestock. A neighbor later told Gray that Zavala was losing his popularity in the area since Emily's arrival. "Unfortunate woman," Gray wrote in his journal, "she is too refined a lady for this sphere." Gray thought the younger Zavala a "sprightly youth" though somewhat short in stature. Lorenzo, Jr., was preparing to join Houston's army as a cavalryman; he would be accompanied by his servant. Even though there was no bed for Gray except blankets on the floor, he slept soundly "under the roof of this remarkable man."

The next morning, March 25, Burnet stopped for Zavala, and the two went by boat to Harrisburg to conduct government business. Burnet wrote all of the letters and issued orders and proclamations, leaving little for Zavala to do.

Zavala was there for four days before he became quite ill; on March 30, he returned home on board William P. Harris' steamboat *Cayuga*.

Zavala was back in Harrisburg in early April when the cabinet was reduced by three: Secretary of War Rusk left for Houston's army, Secretary of the Navy Potter was in Galveston, and Secretary of State Carson started to the United States because of illness. Burnet made Attorney General Thomas acting secretary of war and made Secretary of the Treasury Hardeman acting head of the state department. The president gave Zavala no emergency assignments. Seemingly, a wide breach had developed, and judging from Burnet's future actions, the president had little confidence in Zavala's intentions.

Word reached the temporary capital on April 12 that Mexican troops were crossing the Brazos River at Fort Bend. Leaving Thomas and Hardeman at Harrisburg to pack government papers, Burnet and Zavala boarded the *Cayuga* to rescue their families. The steamer had in tow a schooner and four open boats filled with local residents. Zavala and his family were in Lynchburg on the night of April 13 and the next day moved to William Scott's home on the east bank of the San Jacinto estuary. Burnet took his wife and two sons to Morgan's Point where Morgan's schooner *Flash* was anchored in the river the same day. All could be swiftly evacuated in case Santa Anna's army appeared.

Emily was determined to return to her home the next morning, April 15, to recover a chest of silver and other valuables. Using a skiff, the servants rowed the couple upstream. Nearing Lynchburg, they met the Lynch family going downriver and learned that Mexican soldiers had reached Harrisburg the night before. What they did not know was that Santa Anna himself was in Harrisburg, intent on capturing Burnet and Zavala. The Zavalas returned immediately to Scott's place.

Santa Anna burned Harrisburg the next day, April 16, and

sent Colonel Juan N. Almonte to capture Burnet at Morgan's. As the cavalry approached New Washington, the Burnets rowed out to the *Flash* and sailed for Galveston Island. The *Cayuga* had already picked up Hardeman and Thomas (who was accidentally killed on board), and it stopped for the Zavalas at Scott's landing. The steamer headed to Anahuac near the mouth of the Trinity where some Harrisburg residents debarked to travel overland to Louisiana. Then the steamboat continued to the island with the cabinet.

Meanwhile, Santa Anna and his troops left Harrisburg for Morgan's Point on April 17. They spent two days resting and looting Morgan's home and warehouses before learning that the Texan army had arrived at the mouth of Buffalo Bayou and was in camp guarding the ferry crossing to Lynchburg. Early on April 20, Santa Anna torched Morgan's buildings and hurried his 600 men along the ten-mile trail to engage Sam Houston's volunteers.

Burnet and the cabinet used the various merchant schooners and warships anchored at the eastern end of Galveston Island as headquarters and shelter for their families while the three steamers—*Cayuga*, *Laura*, and *Yellowstone*—served as transports. The only structures on the barren island (previously forbidden for settlement) were the 1832 Mexican customs house and warehouse. Close by, Fort Travis was under construction, supervised by Colonel James Morgan. Civilian refugees from the Brazos and beyond huddled in tents and huts made from flotsam near the fortress.

Burnet's government was in disarray. Zavala's friend from Paris, H. Baradére, wrote from Galveston Island on April 26 to a fellow publisher in New Orleans that, "Irresolution, weakness, divergence of opinion and contradictions marked his government's every movement." Zavala later told Poinsett that Burnet was the most frivolous, presumptuous, and ill-informed man in high office whom he had ever known. All he did was compose bombastic speeches full of meaningless phrases. Under these conditions the frustrated vice president addressed a note to the "President & Cabinet" on April 22:

> Persuaded that my Presence in the Cabinet at present will be of but little service & that I can better employ my time in other services of my country I beg leave to tender my resignation . . . for reasons which I will explain to Congress & the Nation.

Burnet responded immediately, expressing his regret at losing Zavala's counsel. Neither man knew that the day before the Texans had achieved a great victory thirty-five miles away on the McCormick farm opposite Zavala's home. After a brief encounter late on the afternoon of April 20 between Mexican and Texan cavalry and an exchange of cannon fire, the combatants withdrew with neither side gaining an advantage. Santa Anna received 500 reinforcements early the next morning; confident that the Texans posed no real threat, he posted no guards and allowed the newcomers to eat and rest. In midafternoon, Sam Houston ordered his men to form a long double line stretching from trees bordering a marsh along the San Jacinto estuary on the east and extending west toward the prairie. Leaving their camp in the trees along Buffalo Bayou, the Texans marched silently toward the Mexican camp about two miles to the south, passing unnoticed through the tall prairie grass in a swale and hidden from the Mexican breast-works by a slight rise. When they were almost upon the enemy, they shouted, "Remember the Alamo!" as they began firing, clubbing, and stabbing the surprised Mexicans. Amid the panic, Mexican officers could not rally their troops, and men fled toward the swamp, where many drowned, while others dashed toward the prairie only to be cut down by Texan cavalry. The Battle of San Jacinto was over in about eighteen minutes. Almost 600 Mexicans died and about the same number were captured. The Texans lost nine men. This victory returned Zavala to the government.

The Texan scouts captured Santa Anna the day after the battle and took him to General Houston, who had been shot in the ankle. Lorenzo, Jr., one of Houston's aides and his official translator, was called to duty. Colonel Almonte, who had spent his youth in New Orleans and understood English, had been captured the previous day. Almonte interpreted for Santa Anna. Houston immediately negotiated an armistice with the Mexican general: in return for his life, Santa Anna would order the rest of his army west of the Brazos to withdraw to Victoria and San Antonio.

Most of the Texas volunteers, of course, wanted to execute Santa Anna immediately, but Houston and Secretary of War Rusk, who had participated in the battle, preferred to use him as a hostage. This chivalrous and diplomatically wise treatment stirred mixed emotions from Zavala's New York friend, Samuel Swartwout, who thought Santa Anna should die. He wrote to James Morgan in June:

> What would Santa Anna have done to Houston, Zavala, the Nobel, the victorious, the amiable, the talented & learned Zavala, had he fallen into his hands with his wife, his darling son, and his innocent children? He would not have spared him . . . I shudder when I think of Gov. Zavala's danger. . . .

Swartwout asked Morgan to tell Zavala that he was remembered in New York as "the purist of patriots," and that he should remain in Texas to be honored and loved.

Texas army doctors had appropriated Zavala's house for a hospital when Houston's men first reached the area on April 19. Lorenzo, Jr., missed the first confrontation between the two armies on April 20 because he had crossed the bayou to his home to visit an ill friend. While there, he inventoried possessions left behind when the family had fled so that a claim might be made for the food, wine, tools, and other things being used by the doctors and the army.

Word about the great victory did not reach the government at Galveston Island until April 26. But three days earlier, on April 23, Zavala and James Morgan, concerned about their property, boarded the steamboat *Cayuga* that was taking supplies and thirty recently arrived volunteers from New Orleans to Houston's army on Buffalo Bayou. After a night spent stranded on Red Fish Reef, the vessel reached the campground early the next morning. While Morgan's property at New Washington was destroyed, Zavala's home was intact.

What Zavala felt when he confronted Santa Anna is left to conjecture, but the meeting must have been difficult for both. Zavala knew a number of the captured officers, including Almonte, and learned that an old friend, General Manuel Fernández Castrillón, had been killed while rallying his troops near the big cannon. Zavala ordered Mexican soldiers to recover the Spaniard's body and take it across the bayou for burial in a cedar grove on a high bank close to his house. No doubt he could find Masonic brothers to conduct a proper ceremony. This was the first burial in the Zavala cemetery.

Zavala remained with the army through May 1 when he, Acting Secretary of State Hardeman, and Rusk sent Burnet a scathing letter. Why had he done nothing since the 26th? The army was idle and without supplies to pursue the enemy. What was to be done with the 600 prisoners? The three refused to accept responsibility for Burnet's poor leadership and they threatened to resign. Quite by coincidence, Burnet arrived the same day on board the 120-foot-long steamboat *Yellowstone*.

By the time the president reached the battleground, the Texans had moved their prisoners a few miles up Buffalo Bayou to get away from the stench of rotting Mexican corpses. Neither Houston nor Santa Anna would order their burial. Burnet was annoyed that Houston, without executive permission, had negotiated an armistice with Santa Anna, saving his life in exchange for ordering his remaining force to withdraw. When the *Yellowstone* took Burnet, Santa Anna, and all the

Mexican officers to Galveston Island on May 7, Burnet tried to prevent Houston from boarding. Burnet had relieved Houston from duty because of his wound, and therefore he was not entitled to be transported on an official vessel. Houston's friends nevertheless carried him on board in spite of Burnet.

Burnet moved his government and his important prisoner from Galveston Island to Velasco on May 10. The Brazos River village had sufficient buildings to house the officials plus Santa Anna and his aides; there also was fresh water and wood, necessities lacking on Galveston Island. Zavala served as translator while the cabinet negotiated two treaties with Santa Anna. On May 14 after many discussions, Santa Anna signed a public document ending hostilities: he would not resume war against Texas; his army would retreat across the Rio Grande (the new unilateral boundary initiated by the Texans); and prisoners and property would be returned. A secret, second treaty, unpopular with most of the cabinet, would return Santa Anna to Mexico immediately, where he was to use his influence to secure recognition of Texas' independence. Zavala and Hardeman reluctantly agreed to accompany the defeated president to Mexico City to negotiate the treaty of recognition. The new secretary of state, William H. Jack, an able lawyer, argued in vain that making a treaty with a prisoner of war violated international law and custom and was useless. Freeing Santa Anna after the crimes he had committed, he wrote, was unthinkable. Zavala remained neutral and wrote to his son that he was making the dangerous trip to Mexico at "great sacrifice" because it "is the best service" he could make for Texas.

Santa Anna and the two commissioners boarded the Texas war schooner *Invincible* on June 1, ready to sail the next morning. Before the vessel could leave, the steamboat *Ocean* arrived with new volunteers under the command of General Thomas Jefferson Green. They augmented local opposition to the impending departure of Santa Anna, and the mob demanded the removal of the terrified Mexican president. Community leaders whisked him across the river to Quintana where they stood guard to prevent a lynching.

Zavala opposed surrendering to the rowdies during a cabinet meeting the next day. He stood alone, however, and in characteristic style gave them a tongue lashing. "A government that takes orders from armed masses is no longer a body politic," he said as he left the meeting. In great anger he immediately penned his second resignation:

> Quintana 3rd June 1836.
> Taking into consideration that the present Government of Texas has lost the moral confidence of the People and is therefore no longer able to carry into effect their measures, I have to tender my resignation as Vice President of the Republic of Texas.

Zavala visited Santa Anna who was again on board the *Invincible* for safety, and the Yucatecan helped Almonte compose a letter in English for the president to send to Burnet. Santa Anna complained that while he had cooperated with the demands of the Texas government in good faith, Texas had not fulfilled its obligations to him. Disgusted by the events, Zavala left Velasco for Galveston and home on June 10 without a final good-bye to his old friend and enemy. Within a few days, Captain William H. Patton of the Texas army, a trusted and compassionate officer, took Santa Anna, Colonel Almonte, and the other aides to remote Brazos River plantations where the unhappy officers remained for the next five months until the newly elected president, Sam Houston, freed them.

In mid-May Zavala had asked the new secretary of war, Mirabeau B. Lamar, to remove the wounded Mexican officers from his home, an undertaking that was finally accomplished by the end of the month. Lamar, who was a writer, was already collecting material for a history of Texas, and talked at length with Zavala. The Georgia native was also in Texas looking for suitable land for a group of investors who had given him $6,000. Lamar agreed to buy Zavala's eleven leagues on the Trinity River; the Yucatecan had transferred title to Emily in January so that no matter what might happen, it was her property. Lamar would pay twenty-five cents per acre—about $12,000—part in cash and the rest by promissory notes.

Zavala spent the summer months on Buffalo Bayou, again suffering with malaria. He had time to contemplate what had happened since he arrived in Texas one year ago. A letter to Mexía just before the proposed June trip to Mexico indicated that he was reconciled and content to be a Texan. He had been torn between "opposing duties and sentiments" but thought that he had satisfied his obligations "*to my new country* [sic]." There was much support in Texas for union with the United States. "I am of the same opinion . . . it will be very difficult for Texas to march alone among the other independent nations." He must have realized by this time that he would be regarded as an enemy of Mexico, even among his federalist friends, and was probably relieved when he did not have to go with Santa Anna. Zavala, like many others, looked forward to quick annexation to the United States, which would ultimately increase the value of the land. Politics in the United States during a presidential election year, however, would doom their hopes.

Burnet's administration and reputation continued to decline during the summer—the obstacles would have been challenging for anyone. At the end of July, according to the established timetable, he issued a call for the September election for president and congress and ratification of the constitution. There was also a straw vote regarding annexation to the United States. Even before the results were known, Zavala was ready to return to the cabinet and to preside over the opening session of the senate where the new government would be installed. His previous resignations were meaningless because there was no congress to accept his retirement nor a way to replace him. Zavala wrote to Burnet on September 11 that he thought he would be strong enough to ride a horse soon, and then he could join Burnet and "exercise my functions as Vice President." Unfortunately, this proved overly optimistic and two weeks later he told Burnet that he was unable to attend the opening session.

The first Congress met on October 3 at Columbia, the only central village with sufficient buildings in which to hold a convention since San Felipe had been burned. When the official ballots were tabulated, Sam Houston and Mirabeau B. Lamar had won the presidency and vice presidency by large majorities. Burnet wrote Zavala on October 14 that he wanted to surrender the government to the new executives as soon as possible instead of waiting until December as provided in the constitution. Burnet was willing to resign, "But my retirement will not answer . . . unless you concur with me, and tender your resignation: for in such case the executive duties would devolve on you." Burnet's obsessive legalisms aside, did he think Zavala planned a coup? Burnet's letter continued: he was sure that "you will cheerfully accede . . . to promote our common object—the good of Texas." If Zavala acted promptly, Burnet added, Lamar could be sworn in at the same time as Houston.

Zavala, as usual, rose to the occasion and wrote immediately to the members of Congress:

> Zavala's Point October 17, 1836
> Sirs: Not considering my services useful as Vice President ad interim . . . on account of the bad state of my health . . . I have the honor to tender my resignation. . . .

Burnet carefully waited until Zavala's resignation was recorded on October 21, then submitted his own the next day. Houston and Lamar took office immediately.

Zavala, concerned about Lamar's arrangements for the purchase of the eleven leagues, took advantage of the courier waiting to carry his resignation to Columbia. He sent Lamar the following reminder on October 17:

> According to your letter of May, I have been waiting your arrival here . . . to perform the deeds of the Lands I sell to you. Now Sir, I beg you to let me know if you will be here, or. . . . that I should go to Columbia.

Lamar delivered his inaugural address as vice president on October 22, and in the closing gracefully praised his predecessor. Through all of his life, "Governor Zavala has been the unwavering and consistent friend of liberal principles and free government. . . . The gentleman, the scholar and the patriot, goes into retirement with the undivided affections of his fellow citizens." Lamar wished that "the evening of his days . . . [would be]. . . .as tranquil and happy, as the meridian of his life has been useful and honorable."

On October 16, the day before he wrote his third and final resignation, Zavala composed a reflective letter in Spanish to his old friend, Joel Poinsett. He had just passed his forty-eighth birthday, he said, and was tired. He had been sick on and off ever since he arrived in Texas. His role as vice president—a position he had not sought but had accepted reluctantly—was a burden. He immediately discovered that Burnet was incapable of leading the new government at its most critical time. Zavala had tried to organize the ad interim offices in efficient and orderly fashion, but nobody listened and Burnet could not delegate authority. The final embarrassment was the collapse of the treaty with Santa Anna.

Three and one-half months after telling Mexía he was happy in Texas, Zavala changed his mind after a miserable summer. Sickness and political disappointments undermined his confidence about Texas opportunities. He must have realized that the increasing Anglo Americanization of Texas doomed his political future.

"I cannot live in Texas," he wrote Poinsett. The climate was destroying his health, and he feared for that of his family. Moreover, he believed "the imbecile Mexican government" would send another expedition to Texas. Both sides would lose, but Mexico would lose the most. These remarks suggest that Zavala still worried about his native land. Did he secretly hope to reactivate his political career there? Evidently very lonely and missing stimulating intellectual companionship, Zavala told Poinsett that he would be coming to visit him soon.

A few days later and feeling better, Zavala and five-year-old Agustín rowed up Buffalo Bayou on an errand or for pleasure. On their way home, the boat overturned about one-half mile upstream from Zavala Point. The father shoved the boy onto the floating boat and managed to reach the shore. Chilled and exhausted by the effort, Zavala developed pneumonia and died on Tuesday, November 15.

Lorenzo, Jr., and the young widow asked four neighbors, probably Masons, to carry Zavala to the clump of cedars overlooking Buffalo Bayou to be buried near Castrillón and David Thomas who had been interred after he accidentally shot himself. Word reached the seat of government at Columbia one week later on Wednesday, November 23. Senator Stephen Everett, a native of New York, a member of the Consultation from Jasper (Bevil's settlement), and a signer of the Declaration of Independence, announced Zavala's death to the Senate. The members voted to adjourn until the next day in respect for his memory. *The Telegraph and Texas Register*, now published on Wednesday and Saturday in Columbia, printed his obituary the following Saturday:

> Died, on the 15th inst. at his residence on the San Jacinto, our distinguished and talented fellow-citizen . . . this enlightened and patriotic statesman. . . . Texas has

lost one of her most valuable citizens... and society one
of its brightest ornaments.

One month after Zavala's death, James Morgan wrote to
Samuel Swartwout in New York: "Poor Zavala is gone, This
World will mourn his loss—Truly a great man has fallen in
Israel—He was virtuous and nice." Morgan added that the
health of the Zavala family was improving.

The Yucatecan's enemies in Mexico reveled in his
demise. One newspaper, however, noted that Mexico did
not lose Zavala at his death, because he had "already
adjured it" by joining the Texans. The editor lamented
Zavala's blindness and the loss of his services. "Zavala was a
man of great talents..." who wrote and spoke with unbe-
lievable facility, buoyed up by his lively imagination. No
doubt he was "one of the most notable men of Mexico."

Zavala was gone but not forgotten in Texas. The second
Texas Navy in 1838 named a new steam-powered troop carrier
after him. Before the Civil War, two villages within the old
Zavala empresario grant carried his name, one in Angelina
County, the other in Jasper. In 1858 the state legislature created Zavala County between San Antonio and Eagle Pass, but
its court town, Crystal City, has a statue of Popeye commem-
orating its agricultural renown, not one of Zavala. The Texas
State Library and Archives in Austin, completed in 1962, and
a number of schools also bear his name. While most
Mexicans see Zavala as a traitor for signing the Texas Declaration of Independence, independent-minded Yucatecans
even changed the name of their state in 1878 to Yucatán de
Zavala and a memorial was erected in Merída.

It is difficult to assess Zavala's influence during his brief sixteen months in Texas. It was a time of great confusion when
many ambitious men endeavored to impose their stamp on
events. Although Zavala had held more varied positions in
government than anybody else on the scene, his legislative,
executive, and diplomatic experience had been in another

place and another culture and therefore irrelevant to most Anglo Texans. It was difficult, if not impossible, for them to believe that a foreigner held the same basic political philosophy as they did.

Zavala, the idealist, led a pragmatic political life and obviously believed in the aphorism that politics is the art of the possible. From Yucatán to Texas, he tried to implement measures to improve the conditions of the residents—including himself. Idealism sometimes gave way to the reality of current events, and occasionally personal ambition clouded his judgement. Hoping to promote federalist goals in Texas in 1835, Zavala had to relinquish that plan to survive economically and politically. Disappointed that Anglo Texans were slow to accept him and to use his political expertise, he nevertheless was willing to do what he could to help in the struggle against Santa Anna and centralism. It is for this reason that Texans should remember the great Yucatecan liberal.

Afterword

Eleven days after Zavala's death, Santa Anna and Almonte, with pardons and letters of introduction from President Sam Houston, started overland to Washington, D. C., escorted by three Texas army colonels. The former Mexican president had requested an interview with President Andrew Jackson, unrealistically hoping for aid in recovering his office. The Texans and Jackson hoped Santa Anna had sufficient influence to carry out the terms of the treaty signed at Velasco. Jackson sent the pair to Veracruz on board a U. S. Navy vessel on January 31, 1837. In Texas, President Houston freed all the remaining Mexican prisoners on April 21, 1837—the first anniversary of his victory.

Emily de Zavala was visited by Vice President Lamar in March 1837 to complete the business concerning the eleven-league grant and a portion of the five leagues on the San Jacinto. He also interviewed her for his proposed history of Texas. After selling some of her possessions to neighbors, Emily left the same month on board the *Flash* to return with her children to New York. She received an allowance from James Treat, merchant and former Mexican vice consul in New York, who had on deposit Lamar's payment for the Texas land. This money, over $9,000, was lost after Treat died in 1840 and his estate was declared insolvent.

Less than one year after Zavala's death, Emily married Henry M. Fock, an emigrant from Hamburg who worked in a German-owned commission house in New York City. It is clear that he presumed she was an heiress with a sizeable estate. Leaving her eldest son, Henry Cresswell de Zavala in school in New York, Emily and Henry Fock and her Zavala children returned to Texas in early 1839 and reoccupied the house at Zavala Point. Fock replaced Lorenzo, Jr., as administrator of Zavala's estate in 1841.

Lorenzo, Jr., began settling his father's estate in January 1838 after a trip to New York to consult with James Treat. Zavala, Sr., had owned stock in the New Washington Association and had expected to receive a portion of the bonus land as empresario from the Galveston Bay Company. However, neither speculation provided funds for the Zavala estate, although claims continued until 1850. Also the Victor Blanco five leagues on the San Jacinto had not been properly recorded at San Felipe with S. F. Austin's agent, and the Zavala heirs could never secure a clear title. Besides the 177-acre homestead, the house, some furniture, and a few farm animals, there was little to claim. Collecting Zavala's per diem and mileage expenses to the Consultation and convention was delayed because the Republic had no funds. Payments for damages and loss of property during the time the house on Buffalo Bayou was used as a hospital also were postponed. Zavala had loaned McKinney and Williams $3,500 in December 1835, but because of the hard times resulting from the Panic of 1837, the firm was unable to pay even the interest. Instead the partners gave Zavala's estate one slave and a Galveston lot with a house to settle the debt; this dwelling was rented for income while the slave worked for Emily. Lorenzo, representing himself and his married sister in Yucatán, divided the meager estate with Henry and Emily Fock and cleared the accounts in September 1841.

Young Zavala returned to Merída in October on board the Texas war schooner *San Antonio*. The Texas navy expected to aid Yucatán rebels who intended to declare independence, but the revolutionaries changed their minds when Zavala's old friend, Quintana Roo, negotiated a peace accord in December. Lorenzo, Jr., remained in Merída where he married and had thirteen children whom he supported by translating documents and teaching French and English. He served briefly in the Yucatán legislature and remained in contact with his Texas kinsmen through 1880. He died in 1893.

Henry Fock died in 1849, leaving Emily with two young Fock sons, who as adults changed their name to Folk. In 1851, Emily married E. D. Hand, a widower with grown children and the owner of a nearby sawmill. Hand died in 1859, leaving Emily a widow again. Emily's three Zavala children married, but her daughter died in 1857 in childbirth. Emily, in her mid-forties, took the infant, Catherine Jenkins, to raise. Her married sons worked as caulkers at a shipyard at Lynchburg to support their families.

When the house at Zavala Point burned in the late 1860s, Emily moved to Galveston where Agustín (now Augustine) and her Folk sons lived. She sold the old homestead in 1878 to her daughter-in-law, the wife of Ricardo (now Richard), keeping the old cemetery in the family. Emily West Cresswell de Zavala Fock Hand died in Houston at the home of her granddaughter, Catherine Jenkins (Mrs. William E. Hutchinson), on June 15, 1882, and her body was taken by boat to the Zavala cemetery.

Augustine de Zavala's eldest daughter, Adina Emilia, born on November 28, 1861, inherited her grandfather's drive and ambition. Raised in an English-speaking household (her mother was an Irish immigrant and her father only five when his father died), she attended the Ursuline Academy in Galveston and later San Antonio when her father moved there for his health. She also attended Sam Houston Normal Institute at Huntsville and became a school teacher in the 1880s. After her father's death, she was primarily responsible for educating her younger siblings. It was she who changed de Zavala to De Zavala, believing it defined the family's aristocratic roots. She also referred to her grandfather as General Lawrence De Zavala around the turn of the century.

Miss Adina is best remembered for her fight to save the

Lorenzo de Zavala

Emily West de Zavala Folk Hand, probably about 1860 (courtesy Center for American History, University of Texas at Austin).

Adina de Zavala, grand-daughter of Lorenzo (courtesy Center for American History, University of Texas at Austin).

Alamo from destruction. She and other San Antonio women organized the De Zavala Society to study Texas heroes, and in 1893 the club became the De Zavala chapter of the two-year-old Daughters of the Republic of Texas.

The women were also interested in preserving historic sites. The state of Texas had bought the Alamo chapel from the Catholic church in 1883, but the rest of the complex—the barracks, convent, and storage rooms once part of the mission—was purchased by a wholesale grocery firm. Miss Adina extracted a promise from the owner in 1892 that her group would have the first chance to bid on the property whenever it was sold.

Wealthy Clara Driscoll joined the chapter and bought the Alamo property in 1904; the following year the legislature purchased the enclave and gave custody to the DRT. Miss Adina and Miss Driscoll differed in preservation plans and their arguments split both the DRT and the Alamo preservationists. History proved Miss Adina correct in her contention that the convent and the barracks were part of the mission property before 1836 and should be saved.

In 1912, Miss Adina organized the Texas Historical and Landmarks Association that placed thirty-eight markers around the state. She inspired others to preserve the Spanish Governors' Palace in San Antonio and east Texas mission sites. In the 1920s, she wanted to move the graves from the Zavala cemetery on what had become the Houston Ship Channel to the San Jacinto Battleground park because of erosion, but her cousin, the son of her uncle Richard, would not allow it. She died in 1955 at age ninety-three, and like her grandfather, is remembered as a person of strong feelings who was willing to work hard to achieve her goals.

Bibliographic Essay

This essay is arranged more or less by the chronology of the narrative so that, in lieu of footnotes, readers can match the sources used for each section.

The basic source for Zavala's political life in Mexico is Raymond Estep's 1942 Ph.D. dissertation, "The Life of Lorenzo de Zavala" (University of Texas at Austin). A meticulous researcher, Estep exhausted primary and secondary Mexican and Texas sources available at that time including official documents, newspapers, and the private papers of pertinent contemporaries. He also had access to Zavala family papers, then in the possession of Zavala's granddaughter, Miss Adina De Zavala, in San Antonio. Most of this collection is now at the Barker Texas History Center, Center for American History at the University of Texas at Austin (hereafter cited BTHC). Estep's footnotes and bibliography are exemplary and will guide the curious to the proper sources. Estep's focus is Mexican politics, which helps Anglo Texans understand Zavala's role there. However, he was not as knowledgeable about the speculations of the Galveston Bay and Texas Land Company or the details of Anglo Texan politics. Those subjects are not as well developed. A Spanish edition of his dissertation was published as *Lorenzo de Zavala: Profeta del Liberalismo Mexicano* (Mexico City: Librería de Manuel Porrúa, 1952). His chapter about Zavala and the Texas Revolution, with a few changes, appeared under that title in the *Southwestern Historical Quarterly*, Vol. LVII (January 1954), 322-335 (hereafter cited *SHQ*).

A second valuable study is María de la Luz Parcero, *Lorenzo de Zavala: Fuente y Origen de la Reforma en Mexico* (Mexico City: Instituto Nacional de Antropología e Historia, 1969), which echoes Estep's thesis that Zavala's reforms paved the way for those of Benito Juarez in the 1850s. Combing the works of nineteenth-century and modern Mexican writers (plus Estep) who praise or vilify Zavala, she analyzes the motives and background of the authors and their resulting works. Although it appears only in Spanish, it is worth long hours with a Spanish dictionary to understand Mexican attitudes toward Zavala.

The Zavala family papers were given to the Galveston Historical Society by Zavala's son, Augustine, when he moved from Galveston to San Antonio, according to the *Galveston News*, November 13, 1874. Letters, financial records, and five bound diaries with two hundred pages dating from 1821 to 1835 were included, along with a dress sword worn at the French court and a Latin volume published in 1643. Unfortunately, these items were replevined by the family in 1889 and taken to San Antonio where heat, dust, insects, careless handling, and perhaps theft or sales resulted in the loss of some documents by 1940 (especially the diaries) when Estep used the collection. Miss Adina de Zavala deposited her grandfather's papers and some of her own at the University of Texas sometime between 1940 and 1952 where they are preserved in usable order at the BTHC. However, only four pages of the diaries remain—November 10-14, 1831. One presumes neither Miss Adina nor her father, neither of whom read Spanish, intentionally destroyed the others because those four would have been likely targets for shredding—revealing the belated marriage ceremony between Lorenzo, Sr., and Emily West. Financial records and a few letters to Zavala give useful details, but several letters from Lorenzo, Jr., reminiscing about his father's life and his own role in translating for

Sam Houston in 1836 are among the most informative documents.

The Zavala genealogy is detailed in José María Valdés Acosta, *A Través de la Centurias*, 3 Vols. (Mérida: Talleres "Pluma y Lápiz," 1923-1931) while the *Enciclopedia de México*, 12 Vols. (Mexico City: Enciclopedia de México, S. A., 1977) is helpful for biographies, events, and places.

Two analyses of background events and Mexican thought about its frontier are David J. Weber, *The Mexican Frontier 1821-1846: The American Southwest Under Mexico* (Albuquerque: University of New Mexico Press, 1982) and Nettie Lee Benson, "Texas as Viewed from Mexico, 1820-1834," *SHQ*, Vol. XC (January 1987), 219-291.

For the 1820s:

Nettie Lee Benson, ed., *Mexico and the Spanish Cortes, 1810-1822: Eight Essays* (Austin: University of Texas Press, 1966) is topical analysis by Benson's graduate students about this significant experiment with parliamentary government. Timothy E. Anna, *The Mexican Empire of Iturbide* (Lincoln: University of Nebraska Press, 1990) focuses on the political problems of the early 1820s, while the old standard, Wilfred Hardy Callcott, *Santa Anna: The Story of an Enigma Who Once Was Mexico* (Norman: University of Oklahoma Press, 1936) still provides adequate coverage in English of the activities of the ambitious friend and enemy of Zavala.

Zavala's role as it relates to Texas in Mexico's constituent Congress in 1822-1823 and Stephen F. Austin's efforts to secure approval of his empresario contract can be followed by documents in Eugene C. Barker, ed., *The Austin Papers*, Vol. I, in the *Annual Report of the American Historical Association for 1919*, 2 Vols. (Washington, D. C.: Government Printing Office, 1924). Two subsequent volumes, Barker, ed., *The Austin Papers*, Vol. II in the *Annual Report . . . 1922* (Washington: Government Printing Office, 1928) and Barker, ed., *The Austin Papers*, Vol. III (Austin: University of Texas, 1927), include some references to Zavala through 1836. Some of the direct quotations are from these volumes. Robert Leftwich's diary and letterbook, 1822-1824, in Malcolm D. McLean, comp. and ed., *Papers Concerning Robertson's Colony in Texas*, Introductory Volume (Arlington: University of Texas at Arlington, 1986), gives details about traveling to the Mexican capital to secure an empresario grant. H.[enry] G.[eorge] Ward, Esq., *Mexico in 1827* (London: Henry Colburn, 1828) has valuable details about travel, the organization of government, and the tribulations of Mexican politics as seen by the British minister.

Joel R. Poinsett continues to draw scholars: J. Fred Rippy, *Joel R. Poinsett: Versatile American* (Durham, N.C.: Duke University Press, 1935) focuses on his diplomatic activities from the U. S. point of view while José Fuentes Mares, *Poinsett: Historia de una Gran Intriga*, 4th edition (México: Editorial Jus S. A., 1964), gives a negative perspective plus reproducing some useful letters. *The Calendar of Joel R. Poinsett Papers in the Henry D. Gilpin Collection* edited by Grace E. Heilman and Bernard S. Levin (Philadelphia: The Gilpin Library of the Historical Society of Pennsylvania, 1941) has good abstracts from documents in the Poinsett collection beyond the microfilm documents cited by Estep. Other letters can be found in Carlos Basel García, *Documentos de la relación de México con los Estados Unidos, noviembre de 1824-diciembre de 1829*. Vol. I, *Poinsett* (Mexico City: Universidad Nacional Autónoma de Mexico, 1983). Andrew Jackson's correspondence with Poinsett's replacement, Anthony Butler, touches on Zavala and on the Galveston Bay land speculations as impediments to the U. S. purchase of Texas. For pertinent documents previously quoted see John Spencer Bassett, ed., *Correspondence of Andrew Jackson*, Vol. IV (Washington, D. C.: Carnegie Institute, 1929). Mary Virginia Henderson, "Minor Empresario Contracts for the Colonization of Texas, 1825-1834," *SHQ*, Vol. XXXI (April 1928), 295-324, discusses the Burnet, Vehlein, and Zavala grants.

For the 1830s:

Lorenzo de Zavala, *Journey to the United States of North America*, trans. Wallace Woolsey (Austin: Shoal Creek Publishers, Inc., 1980), allows those who cannot read his *Viage a los Estados-Unidos* (Paris, 1834) in the original to understand what Zavala saw and thought about the United States in 1830. Zavala's romance with and marriage to his second wife are detailed in Philip Paxton, *A Stray Yankee in Texas* (New York: Redfield, 1853), 189-190; records of the Church of the Transfiguration, New York City; Zavala diary and Lorenzo de Zavala, Jr., "Memoria de Senor Don Lorenzo de Zavala," in the Lorenzo de Zavala Papers, BTHC.

Several articles in English detail the activities of Zavala's federalist friends. C. Alan Hutchinson, "General José Antonio Mexía and his Texas Interests," *SHQ*, Vol. LXXXII (October 1978), 117-142, is an excellent biography, except Hutchinson was unaware of the way native Mexicans abused the state colonization law and of how Mexía manipulated his purchases (p. 125). Hutchinson's articles about the Mexican federalists in New Orleans in 1835 are particularly useful. See "Mexican Federalists in New Orleans and the Texas Revolution," *Louisiana Historical Quarterly*, Vol. XXXIX (January 1956), 1-47, and "Valentín Gómez Farías and the 'Secret Pact of New Orleans,'" *Hispanic American Historical Review*, Vol. 36 (November 1956), 471-489. Eugene C. Barker, "The Tampico Expedition," *SHQ*, Vol. VI (January 1903), 169-186, remains the standard for Mexía's ill-fated attack in November 1835 but needs revision.

Similarly, Barker's *The Life of Stephen F. Austin: Founder of Texas, 1793-1836* (Austin: University of Texas Press, 1969) gives an overly complimentary view of the empresario's activities but is useful for what was happening in Texas. Barker has a few uncomplimentary remarks about the New York land speculators. Kate Roland Mason, "General John Thomson Mason: An Early Friend of Texas," *SHQ*, Vol. XI (January 1908), 163-198, permits a glimpse of her father's activities for the Galveston Bay Company. The anonymous account, *A Visit to Texas in 1831*, third edition (Houston: Cordovan Press, 1976), appeared first in 1834 exposing the speculators as defrauders of the public. David Woodman, Jr., *Guide to Texas Emigrants* (Waco: Texian Press reprint, 1974), was published in Boston in 1835 to reassure immigrants with favorable details about the Galveston Bay Company and includes an 1830 letter from David G. Burnet. Burnet's efforts to sell his empresario contract between 1827 and 1830 can be found in his papers at the BTHC. Andrew Forest Muir, ed., "The Union Company in Anahuac, 1831-1833," *SHQ*, Vol. LXX (October 1966), 256-268, was the first to use the extensive depositions in the Mexican War claims files at the National Archives that reveal how the New York speculators operated. Muir's papers at Rice University in Houston contain many typescripts of the official documents; similarly, the John A. Rockwell Papers, BTHC, has copies of similar but different documents. Andreas Reichstein explored those files in the National Archives in greater depth to blast the land speculators in *The Rise of the Lone Star: The Making of Texas*, trans. Jeanne R. Willson (College Station: Texas A&M University Press, 1989). His chapter 7 gives an oversimplistic economic determinism view about land speculating, echoing the sentiments of Elgin Williams, *The Animating Pursuits of Speculation: Land Traffic in the Annexation of Texas* (New York: Columbia University Press, 1949). Although contemporaries in the 1830s criticized land speculating, it was usually sour grapes from those who failed to secure wealth. Modern historians, from Barker through Reichstein, absorbed progressive reform movement attitudes during their studies and condemn eighteenth- and nineteenth-century entrepreneurs without walking in their moccasins or breathing the air of the past.

James Morgan and the New Washington Association are also among claimants in National Archives files, and a large collection of Morgan's papers are at the Rosenberg Library, Galveston. In addition, Feris A. Bass, Jr., and B. R. Brunson, eds., *Fragile Empires: the Texas Correspondence of Samuel Swartwout and James Morgan, 1836-1856* (Austin: Shoal Creek Publishers, Inc., 1978), provides a convenient means of reading the difficult handwriting in the collection plus notes and an index.

For a revisionist look at eleven-league land speculating by Austin and his associates, see Margaret Swett Henson, *Samuel May Williams: Early Texas Entrepreneur* (College Station: Texas A&M University Press, 1976). Henson also explains how the land grants were made along the lower Trinity River and the trouble over customs collecting in 1831-1832 in *Juan Davis Bradburn: A Reappraisal of the Mexican Commander at Anahuac* (College Station: Texas A&M University Press, 1982).

Paul D. Lack, *The Texas Revolutionary Experience: A Political and Social History, 1835-1836* (College Station: Texas A&M University Press, 1992), is revisionary in outlook. Lack examines the motives, talents, and rivalries of the men who served in the General Council, Consultation, Convention, and the ad interim government and destroys many myths of the past. Margaret Swett Henson, *The History of Baytown* (Baytown, Texas: Bay Area Historical Society, 1986), and Henson and Kevin Ladd, *A Pictorial History of Chambers County* (Wallisville, Texas: Wallisville Heritage Park, 1988), both fully footnoted, reveal the activities of tories, including David G. Burnet, along the San Jacinto and Trinity rivers. Both books detail events in the area during Zavala's residence.

Henson, "Tory Sentiment in Anglo-Texan Public Opinion,

1832-1836," *SHQ*, Vol. XC (July 1986), 1-34, reveals the division of opinion from the Brazos to the Trinity at the time Zavala arrived in Texas. David B. Edward, *The History of Texas, Or the Emigrants . . . Guide . . .* (Cincinnati, 1836, republished Austin: Texas State Historical Association, 1990), is a treasure of tory reasoning centered at Gonzales. A new analytic introduction puts Edward in perspective. Henson, "Politics and the Treatment of the Mexican Prisoners after the Battle of San Jacinto," *SHQ*, Vol. XCIV (October 1990), 188-230, explains in detail what happened to the privates, the officers, and Santa Anna and his aides based on Texan versions and the published Mexican officer's reports.

Jim Dan Hill, *The Texas Navy in Forgotten Battles and Shirtsleeve Diplomacy* (Chicago: University of Chicago Press, 1937; reprint Austin: State House Press, 1987), remains the best narrative for ships, battles, and policies between 1835 and 1844. Newspapers in Texas and New Orleans report the arrival and departure of commercial vessels between the two. Foreign vessels (including those from Texas) had to register passengers and cargoes at the customs house in New Orleans, and extant passenger lists are available on microfilm.

Two keen observers in 1835-1836 have published diaries. *Mary Austin Holley: The Texas Diary, 1835-1838*, ed. J. P. Bryan (Austin: University of Texas Press, 1965), provides descriptions and sketches of the lower Brazos River made only two months before Zavala arrived. *From Virginia to Texas, 1835: Diary of Col. Wm. F. Gray* (Houston: The Fletcher Young Publishing Company, 1965), gives details about San Felipe, Washington (and the convention), Harrisburg, Zavala's home, and Lynchburg between February and April 1836. Edward N. Clopper, *An American Family* (Cincinnati: privately published, 1950), is a narrative of the Clopper family (who were related to Burnet by marriage) but also provides letters, including one from Andrew Clopper to his father, January 2, 1836, telling of Zavala's arrival. John H.

Jenkins, ed., *The Papers of the Texas Revolution, 1835-1836*, 10
Vols. (Austin: Presidial Press, 1973), is a convenient com-
pendium in spite of its typographical and editorial errors; if
doubt exists, Jenkins provides the location of the original documents. Many of the Burnet and Zavala quotations in this
text are from these volumes. Charles Adams Gulick et al.,
eds., *The Papers of Mirabeau Buonaparte Lamar*, 6 Vols.
(reprint Austin: Pemberton Press, 1968), contains information
about Zavala noted by Lamar while interviewing Zavala and
his wife. Amelia W. Williams and Eugene C. Barker, eds.,
The Writings of Sam Houston, 1813-1863, 8 Vols. (Austin:
Pemberton Press, 1970), has the vituperative newspaper
exchange between Houston and Burnet in 1841 during the
presidential campaign when Houston charged Burnet with
being a tory in 1836 (Vol. 2: 385-386). Gifford White,
Character Certificates in the General Land Office of Texas
(Baltimore: Genealogical Publishing Company, 1985),
abstracts names and dates of those entering Texas including
Lorenzo, Jr., in 1835. Harris County deed, marriage, probate,
and tax records contain many details about Zavala's home
and its ultimate fate along with Mrs. Zavala's subsequent mar-
riages and those of her children. Galveston County deed
records add more details about Zavala's estate. The population schedules of the United States Census, 1850-1880, for
Harris, Galveston, and Bexar counties list Zavala's widow and
her descendants. The Texas State Archives has petitions and
claims from Zavala's heirs for his service at the Consultation
and Convention and the damages and losses to his home
when it was occupied by Texas army surgeons.

Index